REVOLUTION THIS TIME

REVOLUTION THIS TIME

Toward A New Africa

W.O. Maloba

AFRICA WORLD PRESS
TRENTON | LONDON | CAPE TOWN | NAIROBI | ADDIS ABABA | ASMARA | IBADAN | NEW DELHI

AFRICA WORLD PRESS
541 West Ingham Avenue | Suite B
Trenton, New Jersey 08638

Cover design: Ashraful Haq
Book design: LiteBook Prepress Services

Cataloging-in-Publication Data may be obtained from the Library of Congress.

ISBNs: 9781569028179 (HB)
9781569028186 (PB)

For the

Youth of Africa

This is your moment; this is your destiny

CONTENTS

AFRICANS AND THE PALESTINIANS' STRUGGLE FOR LIBERATION

I

On principle, and in fervent opposition to oppression and discrimination, we as Africans, we as people of African descent, must declare our never-ending support of the Palestinians in their struggle for national liberation. In word and deed, we must affirm our solidarity with the Palestinians in their struggle against Israeli occupation, oppression, and humiliation. In this matter, and on this question, there is really no other option. We, more than any other people, should—and must—be sensitive to questions of oppression, discrimination, and humiliation. We cannot at any point confuse oppressors with liberators. Our sentiments and efforts must forever stand in solidarity with the oppressed. To this end, therefore, we must seek to distance ourselves from any cultural or other rationale produced in order to confuse us and steer us away from our chosen solidarity with the oppressed. As Africans, we have never benefited from aligning with the oppressors. On this specific question, it is worth to inquire about our source of information on the Palestinian struggle. Is it the same source that we have relied on in the past—and in the present—for information about communism?

From March 2018 to December 2019, Palestinians in the occupied territories launched demonstrations of resistance against the brutal and discriminatory occupation of these lands by Israel. They were not the first nor the last of these demonstrations of resistance. Over the course of many decades, and especially since 1967, there have been several such demonstrations of resistance by various Palestinian groups.

As in the past, the Western media chose to label these efforts at nationalist resistance by Palestinians as mere "riots." This characterization robs such demonstrations of any purpose and reduces them to unruly mobs, bloodthirsty homicidal mobs consumed with irrationality and menace. Language matters, especially in describing and analyzing instances of nationalist resistance. By labelling acts of nationalist resistance as mob riots, the occupying force finds rationale and cover for brutal response. After all, if these are mob riots, then force is necessary to restore order and normalcy. In this way, brutality is sanctioned and elegantly explained away.

Coverage of these acts of resistance in the Western media is linked to language in the form of newspapers, TV, and various means of electronic communication. For, let us face it, if these acts of resistance are viewed as illegitimate and the actors as crazed homicidal maniacs, then the tone is set for the resultant coverage. As far as possible, there is a lot of emphasis on the mob nature of those engaged in the resistance—their eyes and loud noises, gestures, menacing looks, and eagerness to avenge. Paragraphs and cameras alike are focused on the visible display of pain and agitation of those engaged in the act of resistance. And to the Western media, governments (and even scholarship), they become, by deliberate design, the face of The Enemy, who must then be justly vanquished and, if possible, eradicated.

It is readily apparent that the Western media (print, TV, etc.) are quick to interview themselves on this topic, and any other news of events in the Global South. And, to a large part, this tendency is also evident in Western scholarship. The West, interviews the West, about demonstrations of resistance by non-Western peoples. This is the highest form of cultural imperialism and arrogance. Non-Western peoples cannot be relied upon to describe, let alone explain, their oppression or circumstances of their existence. It is taken for granted that the appropriate knowledge and explanations will issue from the mouths, pens, and hands of the oppressor, as if only the centers of the empire have appropriate knowledge, theories, and solutions. Imperialism not only oppresses and exploits dominated peoples; it also constantly dismisses their mental ability.

The inescapable historical background to these constant demonstrations of resistance is avoided; it is never mentioned or discussed in earnest. There is an occasional brief superficial hint to history, but this is promptly dismissed as irrelevant and, at any rate, not germane to the matter at hand. History of the oppressed, it turns out, is seen as irrelevant in discussing the origin and growth of nationalist resistance. Oppressors have history, while the oppressed have distorted myths and incidents. It is the present that is routinely (partially) discussed, never the troublesome historical background. This avoidance denies these acts of resistance any legitimacy and purpose. And without legitimacy, what we have on the screen and in print, are acts of unprovoked, malicious, and murderous mobs. Once dismissed, these acts of resistance must be quickly and brutally suppressed and negated. Again, language matters. The oppressed cannot find themselves and their causes and objectives in the vastness of the Western media.

To the Western media, non-Western peoples and societies have no legitimate grievances against imperialism; no legitimate causes to fuel their anger, frustration, and resistance. Are the Palestinians really a separate people? Do they really have any concept of a separate national identity? And what does that mean? Who are they anyway? The Western media takes it as an article of faith, solid faith, that in order to be rational, the non-Western peoples, the oppressed and occupied peoples, must willingly and continually accept their assigned lot of poverty and powerlessness. They should be obedient, loyal and even grateful servants. Anything outside these roles is immediately deemed illegitimate and suspect.

Beyond this, there is the agonizing matter of the value attached to the life of the oppressed and the value attached to the life of the oppressor. The playbook of imperial operations stipulates, again and again, that the life of the oppressor is infinitely more valuable than the life of the oppressed. The life of the oppressed is understood to be worthless. The oppressed are seen as permanently disposable people—a multitude of worthless people who can be killed again and again, maimed again and again, without mercy or restraint. There is no punishment meted out, as deterrence, to the oppressors for their repeated acts of violence against the oppressed. And as the oppressed are disposed of, international opinion turns away. There is, of course, the obligatory condemnation of all violence. It is nonetheless widely known that such condemnations are perfunctory and, therefore, worthless. In the case of Israel, we know that it has not been subjected to any real and verifiable international sanctions for its actions. No economic or political sanctions aimed at punishing it for repeated disregard of international accords and for constant violations of the rights of the Palestinians. On this matter Israel has been, in effect, routinely exempt, justified.

By continually supporting Israel, under any and all circumstances, the West, and especially the USA, affirms that indeed it places little value on the lives of Palestinians as a people. No amount of elegant explanation or voluble denial can blot out this haunting reality.

What is disturbing here is that the conservative rulers of the Arab world have in fact endorsed this position: this imperialist position. Conservative rulers of the Arab world have, through their actions and evasions, endorsed the poisonous Western notion that Arab lives do not matter. The conservative rulers have managed to erect walls of separation between themselves and this conflict. After all, they argue, Western governments treat them with respect, bank their money, educate their children, manage their economic enterprises, protect them from local stirrings toward radical change and challenge, and receive their kings, royals and rulers with pomp and circumstance whenever they visit Western capitals. To the conservative rulers, pomp and circumstance is living evidence of equality.

But this is fiction, a disturbing and disabling fiction. It cannot hide the fact that every time the homes of Palestinians are destroyed, children killed, infrastructure destroyed, every time the Israeli tanks roll into Palestinian refugee camps, every time the jets bomb homes and the inhabitants cry in anguish, every time harm and destruction is inflicted again on the Palestinians, every time the Western world walks gingerly and hesitantly to condemn Israeli aggression, every time the Palestinians are roundly and loudly condemned for not exercising restraint, every such time, there is collective humiliation of the Arabs. The West's standard response to Israel's punitive expeditions into the occupied territories is an affirmation of power, the power of the powerful over the ruled, the dominated. The oppressed, the dominated, are forced to absorb the guided and directed fury of the powerful and then deal with their own powerlessness.

It is one of the most unsettling questions of history that the West has managed to oppress and exploit Arabs at a time when opportunities abounded for a genuine Arab realignment, reassertion, and redefinition, both locally and internationally. For what has all that wealth from oil fundamentally accomplished? A classic case of the rulers cooperating in the continued subjugation of their own peoples and societies. The age-old question of collaboration.

The hesitation of the wealthy Arab rulers to forcefully engage in the Palestinian question has to be seen as a mark of weakness on social, political, and even economic fronts—a betrayal of their own peoples and societies in order to uphold an oppressive class structure dependent on the West for support, survival, and safeguard. Yet, it is fair to conclude that consistent defiance by the conservative rulers to continue to plunder and oppress their people will, of necessity, accelerate the rise of national liberation. It would be an extraordinary error, based on self-serving speculation, to continually hold onto the notion that the social, political, and economic structures in these conservative countries are destined to last.

These conservative Arab rulers have, in effect, entered into a functional conspiracy against the progress of their own peoples and societies. By relying on Western imperialism to uphold their positions, intact and unaltered, these rulers see their future in London, Washington, Paris, Berlin, etc. and not in the energy and initiative of their peoples and societies. They are, in effect, the local viceroys on behalf of imperialism, with the assigned task of beating their subjects into obedience and service—common subjects, worrisome people, who must be relentlessly supervised, directed, of course punished, and instructed, forever identified as an ever-present danger to the viceroys and imperialism. Possible actions of resistance by the subjects, even rumored ones, are suppressed and violently put down. To the viceroys, any possible actions of resistance are feared, to be marked for unsettling, gratuitous violence, mis-guided ignorance, and destruction.

This reality, this preoccupation, inevitably limits and conditions their responses to the Palestinians' struggle for liberation. These rulers cannot afford to align themselves, in any forceful and determined way, with this struggle. For to do so would immediately expose them to painful contradictions that abound in their countries. It would also immediately jeopardize their fruitful connection to and alliance with Western imperialism. They cannot support a democratic, egalitarian, anti- imperial liberation of the Palestinians without opening their repressive societies to similar demands for liberation. And for all the talk and posturing, the West does not support truly democratic and egalitarian systems in these countries. The West certainly does not support anti-imperialist nationalist agitations for liberation.

The lessons of the past struggles against imperialism speak loudly and clearly: you cannot cooperate with imperialism and achieve your own freedom, dignity, and sovereignty. There are no viable examples to parade out to support this most untenable thesis. What is known is that collaboration with imperialism leads to painful and shameful stagnation. Such collaboration leads to endless studies that reinforce capital, technical, and even political dependency. Studies, ordinarily undertaken at the behest of Western governments and funding agencies, evade or avoid pointing to imperialism (in all its guises) as the key source of poverty, humiliation, national lack of coherence, cultural disintegration, mismanagement, confusion, squabbles, and stagnation.

II

In response to the Israeli disproportionate use of force leading to hundreds of dead Palestinians, President Trump of the USA chose to side with the oppressor. He openly voiced his open support for Israel in its military operations. As if this were not enough, Trump then announced with flourish that the USA would move its embassy to Jerusalem. A definite provocative act meant to appease his political base, the arch-conservative Jewish lobby close to him, and of course the government of Israel. No other US administration had gone this far. They all supported Israel in its military operations against the Palestinians, but they held back from endorsing the moving of the embassy to Jerusalem. Trump's action signified a conscious, scornful disregard of the Arabs, for this has always been a sensitive matter to them.

The jubilant reception of Trump's flourish action in Israel, especially by the Netanyahu government, demonstrated once again that, in reality, neither Israel nor the West have any desire to arrive at a reasonable solution to this conflict in the foreseeable future. The solutions offered, and then forever modified and then subjected to further modification and redefinition, essentially ask the Palestinians to accept the status quo, and then to also renounce all efforts at resistance to oppression and discrimination. These solutions amount to urging the Palestinians to surrender. Peace imposed by the powerful in which the powerless swear to forego any and all resistance. A statement that restates that the

Palestinians are weak and will never be allowed to reclaim their liberation and dignity.

Over the years of constant warfare, Israel has come to adopt what can be termed the compound strategy of superficial flexibility. This allows Israel to bomb and destroy Palestinians' homes, infrastructure, and occupy parts of the destroyed lands and spaces. And then as a sign of flexibility, it agrees to withdraw its forces from lands and spaces that it was not supposed to occupy and destroy, lands that do not belong to it. This withdrawal is usually accomplished after much fanfare and shuttle diplomacy. In the past, this has involved US envoys flying from one Arab capital to another and then to Israel. The withdrawal, usually partial withdrawal, which is then pointed to as a sign of flexibility and good will, does not in reality move the peace process forward. Before and after the withdrawal, Israel does not deviate from its core objectives—no meaningful negotiation, no recognition (in any consequential way) of Palestinians' demands endorsed by international accords, and always and permanently portraying the Palestinians as murderous thugs and terrorists. In recent period, Israel has abandoned any pretense toward withdrawal. Instead, there has been encroachment, expansion, annexation.

The frequent destruction of the homes, businesses, and infrastructure of the Palestinians, also serves a strategic objective. The Palestinians are forever starting over; they rebuild, and their efforts are laid to waste, the result of Israeli destruction of rebuilt structures. In this way, the Palestinians are forced to be preoccupied with rebuilding what was, with immediate survival; and even that is not assured. Constant destruction of infrastructure and homes is meant to militarily disrupt and seek to destroy heroic sowing of seeds of liberation on the ground.

The strategy of superficial flexibility foresees no end to the conflict. It is a stalling tactic. But as a bedrock of Israel's military and political strategy, it lacks imagination, especially about tomorrow. It is a strategy of decidedly diminishing returns. This strategy can only be seen as viable if it is assumed that the oppressed Palestinians have no memory to sustain their future resistance and struggle for national liberation. The strategy also relies heavily on the overwhelming support of the Western world for Israel, especially the USA. This support by the USA and other Western countries has ensured that Israel does not pay any price for its defiance of international accords on this matter. And, also, that it is provided with a continuous supply of lethal weaponry to give it a permanent military edge over its neighbors. In the case of the USA, there is also substantial annual economic aid to Israel. The rest of the countries, heavily dependent on the West for economic aid and technical support, cannot dare take positions contrary to those held by their masters. It can therefore be argued that the diplomatic support for Israel from the rest of the countries outside the West, is linked to their dependence on the West. But is it realistic to imagine that all these factors will continue to favor Israel, in the foreseeable future? This is a commodity with a very limited shelf life. Up to now, it has created in Israel a state of permanent secure insecurity.

All indications are that the future will look markedly different from today, especially in international relations and ideological alignments and then international political economy. An assertive Global South will not endorse the strategic calculations of the Western-dominated world that has been tilted against the poor and oppressed peoples and societies. This future will also see the rise of democratic and populist systems of government in the Arab world. What is now evident is that, in reality, Israel, the USA, and the West, and the conservative Arab regimes, all abhor the rise of populist democratic regimes in the Arab world. Imperialism cannot advance its agenda of permanent dominance and subjugation if the Arab world is governed by populist democratic systems and governments. It is difficult to see how such governments, obviously responsive to populism and social justice, including Pan-Arabism, can continue to endure this state of affairs of constant Arab humiliation at the hands of the West and Israel. On matters of resistance against imperialism, the constant reality is that the needle only moves in the West when the ground is on fire in the periphery. All the history of anti-imperial struggles has constantly affirmed this position.

For a long time now, Israel has continued to enjoy a decided military superiority over its neighbors, not to mention the occupied Palestinians. This military advantage and elastic support from the West, especially from the USA, has ironically made Israel quite vulnerable in the long run. The country has over relied on its military and has, unfortunately, not been able to develop its diplomatic foundational skills of survival in its neighborhood. It has behaved and acted as a European country in the Middle East. But is it? Can it survive and prosper in peace and security, on a long -sustained basis, as a European country in the Middle East? This is a fundamental question. Are Israeli ad hoc intelligence forays and disruptions in conservative Arab countries enough?

The constant resort to excessive force by Israel against the Palestinians hides one essential reality: Israel lives in a state of panic and fear. The hope and calculation continue to be that overwhelming force will act as a formidable deterrent and scare off its adversaries, especially the Palestinians. But force cannot be a permanent effective weapon. After some time, it ceases to scare, to threaten, to be regarded as too formidable to stand up against. After repeated use, it loses its blinding power and ability to inspire "shock and awe." It just becomes ordinary; harsh and brutal, but ordinary. Further, the loss of life inspires others to enter the struggle, fully aware that such militant efforts might lead to death. How does Israel permanently scare a people who are not afraid to undertake death in the pursuit of their liberation? Is killing them by the hundreds and then thousands upon thousands the answer? Is constant economic blockade against the Palestinians the answer? How long can these multiple strategies be sustained? What is the total aggregate impact of all these constantly contradictory positions?

Lessons of history alert us to the fact that force alone, even overwhelming brutal force and power, cannot deliver peace and security, nor effectively squelch the persistence and power of nationalism. The power of Israel includes nuclear weapons. It is now common knowledge that Israel has atomic bombs in its arsenal. In the development and expansion of its nuclear weapons,

Israel had a long and mutually beneficial economic and strategic alliance with Apartheid South Africa. Indeed, Israel helped "the apartheid state to develop more advanced components of its nuclear arsenal. These two isolated states formed an alliance that allowed South Africa to develop advanced nuclear missile technology and provided Israel with the raw material and testing space it needed to expand its existing arsenal of missiles and nuclear weapons" (Sasha Polakow-Surasnsky, *The Unspoken Alliance: Israel's Secret Relationship with Apartheid South Africa*, London/New York; Pantheon Books [2010]: 7, 39-214). At the height of the anti-Apartheid struggle in South Africa, Israel stood with the white racist oppressors. It not only maintained a very close relationship with Pretoria, but also shared its rationale for racial discrimination. The lucrative economic and technical alliance was further strengthened by an ideological congruity on questions of race and racial discrimination. Leading members of the Likud Party in Israel "shared with South Africa's leaders an ideology of minority survivalism that presented the two countries as threatened outposts of European civilization defending their existence against barbarians at the gates" (Polakow-Suransky: 8, 39-214). Current policies by the Israeli government toward the Palestinians have not deviated from this position of racism and discrimination.

Yet the uncontested possession of nuclear weapons has not in any fundamental way increased the security of Israel. Can Israel use its nuclear weapons against its neighbors or against the Palestinians, and survive intact as a society? What would be left to defend after such detonation? And, indeed, after the detonation, who would be left standing with Israel?

To this extent, therefore, Israel and its bombs is, in Mao's memorable phrase, "a paper tiger"—visibly terrifying, but, in reality, weak and fundamentally ineffective on a long-term basis: "All reactionaries are paper tigers. In appearance, the reactionaries are terrifying, but in reality, they are not so powerful. From a long -term point of view, it is not the reactionaries but the people who are powerful" (Mao Tse-tung, *Quotations from Chairman Mao Tse-tung*, New York: Bantam Books, 1967, p. 39). Right now, Israel has a decided monopoly of nuclear weapons in the region. But will this remain true tomorrow? And, if not, how will the possession of such weapons by multiple countries enhance security, including Israel's security, in this volatile region? Up to now, the West and Israel have facilitated and favored a dysfunctional Arab world: not united, weak, even selfish, continually squabbling with no technologically advanced country or countries with strong nationalist military forces. Does Israel's security have to be at the expense of the security and development of its neighbors, and especially the nationalist aspirations of the Palestinians? Is it to be assumed that Israel will continue to roar and strut without effective restraint, assured of its comfortable spot on the broad shoulders of the American eagle? And what does this multiple dependency on the USA, even with accompanying strut and roar, ultimately mean for Israel's long-term identity and definition?

After every Israeli military incursion into the occupied territories, its generals and political leaders have spoken with bombastic bravado, which surely fuels more resentment of and resistance to the occupation.

The Israeli politicians standing next to the generals have routinely indicated their readiness to respond even more harshly in future, which they do. But their harsh words, swagger, and bravado, in essence are all dismissive of a need for serious negotiations leading to a resolution of the Palestinians' nationalist struggle. The bravado is meant to advertise the power of Israel to subdue and humiliate every presence of the Palestinians. The inescapable fact here is that both the Israelis and the Palestinians have to be seen as populations with legitimate concerns and questions.

Up to now, Israel has enjoyed a disproportionate share of attention, good will, and support at the international level, certainly in the powerful Western countries. The Palestinians, on the other hand, have not had a corresponding level of support in powerful Western capitals. The Western powers have not been even-handed. They have not supported the quest for national liberation of the Palestinians with vigor and verifiable consistency. There can be little doubt that this differential in support affects how this conflict is projected, assessed, studied, and analyzed. It also affects the nature of the prescriptions offered as possible solutions. Linked to this has been the freezing-out of honest intellectual debate and reflections about this conflict in academic circles (including strategic studies), and the mainstream media. Questions surrounding this conflict have been treated as truly "untouchable." Dare to present any detailed analysis of the conflict at your own peril. Raise questions about this conflict at your own peril. This has not been helpful to advancing and expanding our understanding of the main dimensions of this conflict. The unfortunate result of this freezing-out of open and honest debate has been forceful recycling of old positions in the media, and even in scholarship; products of patrolled scholarship which are then eagerly recycled by public intellectuals affirming the same. In the end, for every four steps forward there have been seven steps backward. That is not progress.

It has become customary for every new government in the major Western countries to dispatch its foreign secretary to the Middle East upon assuming office. This is especially true in the USA. The Secretary of State flies to Israel and then to the other Arab countries deemed relevant to the conflict by the USA. And there are the obligatory statements issued promising (sometimes vowing) to move the peace process forward. That the USA is committed to finding a workable and honorable peace in the Middle East. This might be followed by a flurry of mini -shuttle diplomacy in the initial years of the new administration, after which there is limited activity and sparse hopeful pronouncements. It is a dance with well-known and well-rehearsed steps. Even when danced with great flamboyance, as was the case with Henry Kissinger, there is little to show at the end by way of concrete advancement toward finding a solution to this matter. Indeed, what, in reality, did Henry Kissinger achieve in the Middle East?

What there is, and what there have been, are a series of improvised ad hoc self-serving engagements leading to ineffective platitudes. Power, Western power, and specifically USA power, ensures that the Arabs (and even the rest of the international community) are expected to pretend that these ad hoc measures represent original contributions and a way forward. But it is clearly evident, as in the past and the present, that these postures on the international stage by successive USA governments are just that: improvised, ad hoc, and not linked to history; not meant to offer any rational solution to the series of problems at the heart of the Palestinians' struggle for liberation. It is almost ritualized engagement (if at all), without positive impact. And so, after every such engagement, after a round of well-publicized shuttle diplomacy by the US Secretary of State, pictures are taken, and the usual platitudes pronounced. There may be even some smiles in the pictures sent across the world. Yet everyone is aware that this sad episode will be repeated tomorrow.

REMEMBERING WINNIE MANDELA

I

Winnie Mandela is dead. And we should all weep for Winnie. As we weep, we should remember that in the difficult days of Apartheid she was banished to the remote rural areas away from her home in Soweto as the Boers sought to minimize her impact and remove her from the charged political scene as an articulate and fierce symbol of the nationalist resistance movement. And to this we must add the numerous instances of violence against her and her children, death threats to scare her into submission, deployment of spies to monitor her activities, resort to malicious smear campaign against her person, efforts at entrapment, and general continuous harassment.

We should start with the obvious: that it was Winnie and her dogged and unflinching efforts that kept the memory of the liberation struggle alive at a time when the ANC was in exile (and not particularly vibrant) and other leaders had been killed by the Boers or were in detention or prison. It was Winnie—firm, dignified, uncompromising, unrelenting—who kept the struggle in the memory of the oppressed in South Africa. And let us face it: the reality is that it was Winnie and her activism, her radical activism, it was this woman, who made Nelson Mandela a household name across the world. Winnie made, or shall we say transformed, Nelson Mandela into the admired and revered symbol of liberation.

After the event, after the fact, there is always the danger of revisionist history. Details are omitted. Stories are altered and meanings are adjusted. The value of individuals and ideas is erased or shelved below away from view. And, of course, the prevailing ideology and emphasis can determine and indicate who should be lauded and who should be shunned, punished, denounced, and denied recognition. The historical period, and its dominant values, are integral in the selection and celebration of individuals. Nonetheless in South Africa, these realities cannot be easily altered and discarded 'in the hearts of the people.' No amount of adjustment of information (including official mandated loss of memory), no efforts to erase or revise the facts, can ever succeed or deny or for that matter eject Winnie from the center stage of the liberation struggle in South Africa.

All of this needs to be mentioned because of the unreservedly critical media coverage that has accompanied Winnie, especially since 1990, and now at the end of her life. From the moment that Nelson Mandela was released from detention, the white-owned and white-dominated media in South Africa, and then the powerful Western media companies, sought and succeeded in portraying her as an unacceptable, out of control black radical opposed to "forgiveness and compromise." Winnie was portrayed as the intransigent (and even dangerous), unyielding black radical unwilling to "forget the past." She became, by deliberate design, the symbol of intolerable black radicalism; the kind of radicalism that sought to open the cover on the pot of Apartheid and look inside for sins, and unforgiveable crimes against humanity—African humanity.

The Compromise forged in South Africa between the guardians of Apartheid's crimes and the ANC (African National Congress) sought cover in one manufactured but officially sanctioned reality: that there shall be no mention, let alone detailed analysis, of history. That history was to be banished and avoided. The Compromise endeavored to portray the problems in South Africa as technical issues, the present and the future as a technical problem indifferent to history. And for this conspiracy against the people of South Africa to take root and work, Winnie had to be sidelined, banished, and then, with vigor, demonized.

And so, all the manufactured as well as the "footnoted crimes" that Winnie has been accused of have to be viewed against this ideological background, with the avowed objective of maintaining racial white supremacy in this "liberated South Africa." We cannot understand the meaning of the persistent savage attacks on her unless we recognize that indeed these attacks are also, in essence, a concerted assault on black radicalism in South Africa. Winnie wanted to open the box of history, for she knew that the ANC Compromise could not survive at all if history was allowed to enter the room. If history becomes the central factor, the defining factor, in the forging of solutions and determining the shape of post-Apartheid South Africa, then the ANC Compromise will inevitably fall down and drown in the contempt and resistance of the people. This Compromise cannot be defended by the long history of oppression and discrimination in South Africa. Winnie articulated the hurt, the anger, and the overall the anguish of the victims of centuries of racial discrimination and exploitation. Winnie's radicalism terrified both the children of Apartheid and the new African rulers; beneficiaries of the Compromise.

As expected, the trumpets of condemnation of Winnie have been sounded most loudly in the West. As part of its imperial mission, the West takes it upon itself to categorize the oppressed. The down -trodden, the despised, the oppressed, the excluded must be described and categorized. The value of the oppressed, that is, the value of the excluded, can only be determined by the West, home of overseers and oracles. And so, in keeping with this imperial mission, which it takes very seriously, the West dutifully and unfailingly picks heroes for us. It picks those to be admired and emulated. Directly or indirectly, these choices also point to the values and characteristics that can earn one a favorable mention, and even a likely consideration for the category of hero. To resist, or to cause others to resist imperialism and its objectives, is to be categorized as an enemy. And then all will be done to diminish your role, your value and importance to your society and to the world. To be good is to submit.

The urge to submit, the lure of submission, is also facilitated by sheer opportunism, if not callous selfish cynicism of the comprador class. And here must be included many of Africa's educated class. There is the fear to contradict. The fear to resist at any level. The tendency to find cover in sophistry and ever extensive footnotes and incomprehensible utterances as signals of knowledge. It is this massive fear, which produces the willingness to submit, that the West counts on to reinforce the imperial system in the Global South. We, the oppressed, even if educated, volunteer to stand guard to protect this system. We are loyal defenders of a system that has never looked at us as anything other than labor: derided and despised labor. We voluntarily patrol the edges of the Global South for would be saboteurs of the system. Willing servants eagerly editing and policing ourselves for imperialism. And so, we rejoice when we are singled out for praise. We are so used to being abused, exploited and despised, that when the master smiles in our direction from time to time, we label this as evidence of progress.

Self-censorship among the oppressed, exploited and despised, remains one of the most powerful and enduring weapons at the disposal of the master. For if the oppressed can police and censor themselves, and in the process avoid coming in contact with threatening theories and opinions, then the imperial system can be assured of some extended existence. Policing the system becomes a shared responsibility. And the few rewards for self-censorship are dangled in front of the comprador class; this includes the self-preservation of the comprador class.

Long before Winnie died, that is at the height of the temporary euphoria that attended the fall of Apartheid, the ANC was already a compromised party; a coopted liberation movement now nominally in power but in reality, presiding over the treasonous betrayal of the majority of the Africans. There was a hurried march from liberation leadership to successful businessmen (mainly), and captains of industry and senior civil servants all sworn to defending the structure of an economic and social system previously devised to uphold Apartheid and discrimination against Africans. The struggle for liberation was against this system. Yet now it was seen by the ANC as relevant, legitimate and the pathway to progress. In spite of the litany of publications issued at the behest of the International Monetary Fund, the World Bank, etc. to provide ideological underpinnings to policies that laughed at the poor and criminalized agitation for social justice, the ANC experienced the steady erosion of its support and the dimming of its star among the Africans.

What Winnie saw, and what informed her post-Apartheid agitation and activism, was the rise of individualized definitions of liberation. The struggle had been collective and national. The fruits of *Uhuru* (freedom) were now calculated on an individual level, and always against the poor, the majority of the African population. She remained committed to the ideals articulated in the liberation struggle. She remembered the many young people who sacrificed so much for the struggle, only to become part of the lost generation; not accounted for in the elegant statements issued by the post-Apartheid ANC. She was appalled by the urge of the new black ruling elite to emulate the former masters, yesterday and today's oppressors and exploiters.

II

Liberation, as the sacred objective of the oppressed, the exploited, evaporates on the horizon the moment political leadership re-directs its attention, focus and justification away from radicalism; the moment political leadership rushes to emulate the master. Emulation of the master and his ways, his methods, his values, have always been a reactionary indulgence. This emulation must inevitably create, or perpetuate, a class of the oppressor and the oppressed, the exploiter and the exploited, the plunderer and the plundered. Appropriate rationalizations, all high sounding with self-serving examples, will be readily produced to justify this arrangement. From far and from up close, what is clear is that this is an old arrangement, there is nothing new here. The master's house has been given a new coating of paint. But the structure remains the same. There was no stoppage of work in the house at all. Local overseers changed shifts, but the machines still run the same as before for exactly the same purpose. To this end, emulation of the master, is death to the oppressed and exploited.

It has become customary in post-Apartheid South Africa, as in many post-*Uhuru* (political freedom) African countries, for academic studies, political narratives, and Western international agencies, to look at the African experience as too varied and complex. "Too complex for words"—an experience (and condition) so multilayered and complex that it would be factually impossible to collapse all these layers into one or even a few categories. An extension of this argument holds that due to these varied experiences and complexities, maybe it is irresponsible to talk of one form of liberation for African people in South Africa (and other African countries). That maybe we should be talking of many liberations; varied small-scale multitudes of rarely interconnecting liberations. On the surface, this may sound like a measured and reasonable postulate. But it is not. It is the kind of unintelligible sophistry that evades any talk of liberation, let alone revolution. It sneers and, with relish, sniggers at any such objective. This argument avoids direct engagement with questions and issues that still haunt the African world and instead finds a home in evasive meanderings, perpetual self-doubt, and insecurity. This is the kind of sophistry that the West and Western scholars can embrace. Quite often, this sort of intellectual output is characterized as "nuanced and sophisticated." It is nonthreatening to imperialism and its supporters. In the African world, we do not have the luxury of indulging in such mystical, and fundamentally escapist, intellectual meanderings.

If we over-subdivide the nature and meaning of the African struggle for liberation, we inevitably end up with unintelligible, incoherent, and fragmented sets of problems, too fractured and divided to be thought of as cohesive, or even coherent, let alone focused. An endless division and subdivision of issues into infinite fractions that end up being everything and, therefore, nothing. And this formless massive nothing, even when accompanied with "nuanced analyzes" and international appeal, has become a beguiling death trap for us, a slippery swamp from which we cannot escape, in order to imagine, let alone plan, the struggle for our liberation. We move from lecture to lecture, conference to conference, book to book, article to article, dismissing the possibility of revolutionary change in Africa; denouncing such advocacy as naïve, gullible, unrealistic, misinformed, and a waste of time. This is also the position held by international funding agencies, Western intelligence agencies, and experts at the imperial center.

In denying the rationale and basis of African liberation, the nature of this struggle is immediately relegated to individual experiences and efforts. Collective identity and class identity are all dismissed as irrelevant and too unwieldy. In this way, every person is theoretically supposed to design and implement their own version of liberation. And everything is done to dissuade people from forming large activist organizations. Such organizations are now seen as oppressive, and as enemies of individual freedom. It is worthwhile to remember that the Western experts who advise the ruling elite in African countries—and massage their egos—abhor the very idea of class as a basis of social organization. They are dismissive of class analysis of issues and societies. And, of course, to them, imperialism does not exist and therefore it has had minimal, if any, impact on Africa's past and current economic and political challenges.

For us in the Global South, we must always remember that Western scholars, journalists, intelligence agents, modern-day explorers, etc. who come for brief visits and then issue weighty pronouncements about us, that these people do not know us, and they really do not wish to know us. They come to see what they have been programmed to see. Their pronouncements are conclusions that they already had in their heads and briefcases, before setting foot here. They are unwilling to study and learn from us, on our terms, as equals. They come with a template, and then with due diligence, seek to fit us into the template. Imperial arrogance ensures that they, these Western experts, etc., can never admit to ignorance or incompetence on their part. The master always knows. The master is always informed.

The success of these experts can be easily seen in the hearty and wholesome embrace of individualism by the African ruling elite, as the basis of the formulation of national economic policies. Now, of course, we know that individualism is seen as an indispensable vehicle for controlling and affirming oppression and exploitation in Western societies. Individualism avoids, resists, and is forever suspicious of solidarity movements, a category that, lately, has come to include trade unions. Also, individualism is skeptical of extensive analyses of issues, including the capitalist system. In this way, therefore, individualism is a strategic digression fostered and nurtured by the capitalist system. On a daily functional basis, individualism acts as the ultimate shield for the racist capitalist system. It exonerates the capitalist system. And this is increasingly true in the countries of the Global South, including South Africa. The system is presented as theoretically flawless and functionally without peer; cumulatively, as a system above reproach. All the policies dictated by the World Bank and the International Monetary Fund, and a multitude of Western economic experts distinctly seek to reinforce this point. This is a perfect building, a perfect structure. Those who fail to enter are to blame for their racial, mental, gender, and/or cultural infirmities.

Winnie's political resistance and activism in post-Apartheid South Africa saw the inherent defect in the imposed economic solutions. These prescriptions had regrettably accelerated, expanded, and deepened the atomization of the country into a society of hostile individuals (and communities). Thus, adherence to the strictures of the Compromise, which centered its policies on individualism (favoring the elite), had to be correctly seen as an elaborate conspiracy against national liberation in South Africa.

The experience of post-Apartheid South Africa, under the stewardship of the ANC, demonstrates again and again the folly of basing national policies on the proposition that the spectacular success of a few individuals will translate to national development. There is no verifiable evidence, as Winnie knew and routinely articulated, to support the theory that an amalgam of several success stories among the oppressed, among the despised, will lead to liberation: to national liberation. The "exceptional native" or "outstanding woman" do not lead to the desired liberation of the Africans. Their presence has generally been converted into a shield of defense by the system, against incisive criticisms. Be patient, progress is coming. Look at the glistening wealth of the new rich. Admire these success stories. You too, can be rich and famous in this system.

Two problems arise out of this formulation. First, the nature and pace of change is set and determined by the oppressors. It follows, naturally, that the oppressors cannot support a pace of change—and, even more crucially, a type of change—that threatens the integrity of their system. And so, the trickling drops of the "exceptional natives" is not, and cannot, be seen as the coming of the collective suicide of the oppressors. No, it is not. Just as in the colonial system, these trickles are meant to undercut the basis of criticisms against the system.

Second, there is a problem about the significance (and conduct) of the "exceptional individuals" among the oppressed and exploited. Their elevation is a strategic proposition on behalf of the oppressors. They are elevated, as is the case in South Africa, in order to reinforce the walls of the system and not to demolish the structure. And we see that these individuals rarely, if ever, question the structure of the system. From time to time, they will utter a mild rebuke at an isolated event that is particularly heinous. But after that mild rebuke, they will retreat to their quiet, profitable corner. If these individuals are taken to be role models, then we have problems regarding the meaning of this symbolism. If the role models signal surrender, how can they possibly be seen as symbols of liberation? Oppressors are adept at understanding the meaning and value of symbolism. For the oppressed, there is a need to dissect and then inspect the contents and intent of such symbolism.

One of the fundamental errors committed by the leadership of the ANC was to allow their vision of society to be determined from outside. The ANC, essentially, ceded the power to define their revolution to outsiders—specifically, the West working in conjunction with the internal white property owners in South Africa.

Subsequent tighter incorporation into the imperial network, even at the flattering level of being labelled as the most developed economy in Southern Africa, did not constitute liberation. History provides no examples of formerly dominated countries (in the Global South) that attained and sustained liberation and development under the guidance of imperialism. In practical terms, imperialism stands at the opposite end of liberation, of freedom, of tolerance, of development, of social justice.

Having ceded this crucial responsibility of defining its revolution to outsiders, the ANC was unable (and unwilling, at all levels) to transform populism into revolution. Africans in squatter camps, the unemployed, workers, landless, young and old, including the lost generation, housemaids, miners, farm laborers—all waited for the ANC to stand up. And, sadly, it could not, it would not. In assuming power sworn to defending the Compromise, the ANC lacked the resolve (and intent) to stand up. All revolutionaries know that populism alone is not enough. If it is not harnessed to a focused revolutionary cause, it can quickly degenerate into empty sloganeering, and then betrayal of the original cause.

All the post-Apartheid activism of Winnie Mandela sought to remind the ANC to retrace its steps back to the original commitment to social change; the promise of revolutionary change that had prompted many Africans to sacrifice their lives for the struggle. The danger, as Winnie saw it, lay in imagining that populism and populist rhetoric and even pronouncements mark the end of the struggle for radical change. Populism and rhetoric alone, it turns out, do not constitute revolution.

DONALD J. TRUMP AND THE "SHIT-HOLE COUNTRIES"

I

The West does not expect the consequences of its mistakes and crimes overseas to follow it home. Mistakes and crimes are denied, re-defined, elevated, characterized, and then lauded with imperial justification. The expectation is that the natives in the Global South will continue to be polite and dutiful to the white *Bwana* (master), obedient and diligent in their service as exploited labor in the empire. It is hoped that the natives will remain where they are in their wretched home countries and that they will not seek to migrate to the center of the empire. Exploited and oppressed people hidden far away from the splendor of imperial spoils. Contradictions of imperialism are not supposed to come to the shores of the West. Massive poverty in the many countries of the Global South, the result of exploitation and plunder, is not expected to give rise to constant extensive migration in search of survival.

On the ground, it is easily observed that economic and military violence against these countries at the hands of the West (and its local allies) has not only destroyed homes, cultures, infrastructure, but also lifestyles, communities, tested methods of survival, and even hope.

These natives who have made the West rich and prosperous over the course of centuries have always been found unfit to enter; they smell, they eat strange foods, they harbor unknown fearsome diseases. Their cultures, languages, and customs are unfathomable and despicable; too incomprehensible. They are different; too dark. And therefore, inevitable enemies of the West.

Imperialism has never admired the exploited and oppressed. To be exploited is to be despised and humiliated. To be exploited is to confirm your assigned low status and therefore to be declared unfit to enter. The poor, the dark ones, those identified as desperate, oppressed, and uprooted, lack credentials for entry and welcome into the haven that is the West.

In 2016 and beyond, desperate refugees from the Middle East, mainly from Syria, started to move to Europe at a steady pace. This migration of men, women, and children, united in misery and barely hanging onto life, gave rise to frantic alarmist media coverage in the West, and even in some parts of Eastern Europe. Indeed, the barbarians were at the gates. It became politically and socially necessary to forget that these refugees were the product of Western military and economic policies of aggression inflicted on countries and peoples of this region with devastating impact over a prolonged period. The historical origin of this migration was sidestepped.

It was inconvenient. Political (and financial) fortunes of European Right-wing demagogues rose as they outdid each other in formulating policies to deny entry to these mostly Muslim refugees. Who could be white and Western and doubt that these refugees were Al Qaeda's fifth column?

Bigoted and racist, these politicians and their many supporters, have paraded themselves as defenders of the West and whiteness, of true whiteness. They have warned of the coming end of the West, the change in the culture, economic status, lifestyle, and whiteness of the West. Settlement of refugees will erode the power and glory of the West, inevitably leading to intolerable and unbearable brownness: the end of whiteness. Isn't it right for whites to defend their homeland from these strange invaders in their midst? Let them go back to their lands weighed down by their chaos, disease, poverty, lack of modern infrastructure, and regressive cultural values. Europe and the West [and now the East] is for whites only; it should be kept for whites only.

But how about whites outside Europe? Should the same principle apply? Should non-white countries be for non-whites only? Would this be seen as acceptable in the West and its racial configuration? Western racist utterances conveniently ignore and overlook the global catastrophic impact of the European diaspora. Invasions, holocausts, slavery, colonialism, white settlers and stolen continents and lands, universalization of racism, the rise and expansion of imperialism, permanence of underdevelopment and poverty, cultural imperialism. The European diaspora is the product of the search for economic opportunities.

Those who migrated were driven by the quest for increased economic opportunities that were wanting in their home countries. When did the USA become a European country? Whose land, is it?

On this same matter, it is legitimate to inquire as to when European immigrants across the globe, and especially in the countries termed "Shit-Hole" countries by Donald Trump, ever considered the impact of their presence on these societies? Did they worry about how these countries would be forever changed, how the texture of their cultures and sense of identity would be so drastically changed? And when they stayed through force, did they ever care about how much they had altered these societies, including their names? Were they ever remorseful, or did they in fact construct elaborate rationalizations to justify plunder, massacres, and even holocausts? Did they ever seek for relationships based on equality, or was white supremacy their sole and driving objective? Can they envision an existence based on equality of peoples?

Trump has never been interested in these weighty historical questions. His pronouncements display a kindred familiarity (and solidarity) with the racist demagogues in Europe, who have now been accorded political respectability by participating in national elections and sometimes winning seats (and power) in national assemblies. The age of newly refurbished and retuned Nazism is upon us. There is no need to hide behind white sheets or in basements. Nazis and their brethren, all so white, can now come out and claim their place at the table.

The matter at hand, as Trump and his supporters (open and hidden) saw it, rested on two main interlocking issues: racial supremacy at home and unimpeded imperialism overseas. The assertion of power, white power, was the loud trumpet that announced the dawning of a new era of unashamed racist politics. Racist politics having dispensed with cumbersome euphemisms.

In exercise of this white power, Trump came to embrace flamboyant gestures, specifically the issuing of proclamations and presidential decrees. While many were non-consequential and several faced endless legal challenges, Trump and his supporters rejoiced in the terror induced by these decrees. They suited Trump's style, for at his core Trump would rather be king than president. He abhors the whole idea of accountability. He resists restraint and believes he is above the law or should be allowed to function above the law. He is, by inclination and self-perception, a dictator—an abrasive and belligerent dictator; spiteful, vengeful, racist, vain, and yes, spectacularly ignorant.

In early 2017, the disastrous effects of Trump's orders banning Muslim migration to the USA, and even visitors, were evident everywhere. Stranded passengers in airports sometimes forced to return to their points of origin, which could be a hazardous undertaking if one is escaping the point of origin. As outcry across the land and beyond mounted, Trump remained defiant, holed-up in the White House, issuing more decrees and spiteful comments against his opponents, while his base cheered.

Trump's defiance and belligerence exposed his intent: to keep the USA and, by extension, Europe, white and for whites only. It was instructive to see discussions about immigration quickly spill over into racist vitriolic rant.

Trump wants to reclaim the USA as a predominantly white country. The presence of non-whites offends his senses, sensibilities, and being but not his economics. He imagines a time when the USA was purely a white country. This is the stuff of fantasy and wishful thinking. For, let us face it, the USA has never been such a country. It has never been a white country. Even if you allow for the near annihilation of Native Americans in their native lands, at the hands of homicidal and plunderous white invaders, you must still account for Africans, millions of Africans, forced into slavery.

What we know is that from the time of the massive landing of Europeans in this hemisphere, these continents of North and South America have been under white domination; that is, white oppression and exploitation. These continents have been held in a sweaty continuous suffocating chokehold of white supremacy. And this white supremacy was formulated and enforced through violence. Thus, violence is intricately integral to white supremacy. Those who were subdued remained in those positions due to the application of violence, or the threat of unspeakable violence. Beyond violence was the whole edifice of discriminatory practices that came to be erected and implemented under the rubric of culture, civilization, and tradition. Those cultural structures in turn justified continued resort to violence to subdue resistance and enforce oppression and exploitation.

The fear expressed by whites in this changing, yet stagnant world, speaks about the past and its implications for the future. Since the 15th century—or, more consequentially, the 16th century—Europeans have dominated world commerce and violence and have, with abandon, exploited and plundered the world outside the West. This is imperialism. In other words, the identity formation of the modern Europeans, and by extension Europeans in the USA, Canada, Australia, etc., has been achieved and retained in the period of imperialism. Thus, they have no other modern frame of reference other than as imperialists. Their power and privileges are all the result of this plunder and exploitation framed in racism. The Atlantic slave trade and slavery, which gave rise to modern racism against Africa and its far-flung children, still shapes the world view of Europeans. And to this must be added all other theories formulated in the European world about race and race distinctions. This is the crux of the matter. Can the sons and daughters of this racist imperial past, renounce it? Can they renounce this plunderous past that has led to this painful racist moment that is intolerable to the majority of humanity? Can they remake and redefine themselves? The problem lies with them and this past that they revere and have sworn to uphold.

Non-white immigration to the USA disturbs Trump's world view in part because of its long-term historical implications. Violated, oppressed, exploited, denigrated, these excluded populations are not only increasing in numbers, but they are also becoming politically and socially vocal; organized, resolute, restive, and now repeatedly insisting on their own definitions. They now define themselves and seek no assistance in displaying these new definitions. The new definitions reinforce the drive toward equality and non-discrimination. The new definitions also seem to doubt the ability of capitalism and imperialism to provide required answers to the knotty social, economic, and political problems.

The drive toward self-definition means that the non-whites no longer defer; they are choosing to struggle for equal citizenship. The struggle signals their refusal to accept their life circumstances as natural and ordained by some inalterable fate. These new definitions indicate their refusal to live and die below the deck. They seek fresh fruits and foods *on* the deck. They are refusing to be the permanent "Other."

This political awakening, this restiveness, born out of courage and unflinching determination, worries the country's ruling classes because of its political and social implications. Will the oppressed seek to uphold the social and economic system that has long denigrated and exploited them? How about the elaborate system of racism? Will the oppressed uphold this system in all of its layers, carefully crafted over centuries to reinforce exploitation? Will the "Other" see merit in this bloodstained edifice? In other words, will the excluded become avid supporters of capitalism and imperialism and uphold white supremacy? Are whites assured of continued supremacy? How can white supremacy be maintained if its foundations are under attack and crumpling? Trump's fears are similar to those that consumed the Boers under Apartheid, leading to eternal panic and worry about the meaning and implications of political and social (and especially economic) equality. Racism that poisons and paralyzes logic and political discussions. Racism that is forever terrified of its own creations.

II

Trump specifically included African countries in the category of "shit-hole countries"—dysfunctional, poor, and wretched countries choking in unspeakable misery: dark countries. Undesirable countries with nothing of value to contribute to the West. Mismanaged countries due to inherent ineptitude of the Africans. Countries with no aptitude for development or modernity. Countries condemned to misery and poverty. Countries with cultures that somehow exhibit continuous hostility to development and five-star hotels. Envious countries longing for what they cannot have due to their own indigenous ineptitude: Western wealth and standard of living, law and order, and the glittering lights in the cities.

Racists of the world have long felt self-assured to insult Africa, Africans, and people of African descent worldwide, because it has been clear to them that their actions would not lead to any material consequences or repercussions: no consequential penalties for insulting and humiliating Africans. Lack of consequences means that Africa and its children worldwide have been the proving ground of racists and bigots. This continent of black people is the universal punching bag. Punch, punch, bite, scold, humiliate, rob, plunder, insult, denigrate. Do all these, and more, and still there are no material penalties whatsoever. It is the land of the weak, the poor, the despised, the dismissed, the oppressed, and the exploited. Poverty and weakness, which are products of past and current imperial domination, have been cited by racists and bigots as evidence of inherent (therefore biological) ineptitude of Africans.

Trump's choice of places to insult and humiliate was therefore deliberate. He punched, even with his reputed small hands, those who could not fight back. From his imperial perch, Trump was fully aware that he could, with impunity, insult Africa and that the rest of the world would either shrug off the matter or at best issue mild, incoherent, and muted statements of disapproval. No firebrand condemnations, let alone threats of economic or political consequences; just mild muted statements of disapproval usually included in a press release dealing with other issues. And here lies the problem.

It has been known for some time to racists and imperialists that responses by Africans to these insults will be constrained by two crucial factors: poverty and self-hatred. Many Africans lead what can only be termed subsistence living; eking out a living in what are surely permanently perilous circumstances. And in this state, under the force and power of colonialism and imperialism, they are of course dependent and weak. This dependence, which manifests itself outwardly as poverty and weakness, compromises their ability and intent to respond resolutely to insults against them and their kith and kin.

Racists also count on the fact that quite a number of Africans and/or people of African descent in the diaspora either share Trump's attitude and diatribe, or secretly think he was correct. This is especially true of the rich, the educated, the elite, who seek to distance themselves from Africa. Association with Africa is seen as injurious to their fame, status and fortune. And so, for these people, Trump's insults have no meaning to or bearing on them. They do not see themselves included here.

They do not belong, and therefore, they cannot be insulted or demeaned. They do not see themselves insulted as members of the "shithole countries." Property, fame, status, fortune, education, and qualifications have given them automatic exemption from inclusion in this humiliating category. How can they be part of this shameful and dreadful category when they have climbed so far, so very high, when they have distanced themselves so much from Africa? There is, therefore, an emotional, psychological, not to mention cultural distance between them and Africa; between them and poor blacks; between them and the African villages.

The seduction of power as well as a yearning to be seen as "successful and cultured" has forced some Africans, African Americans, and other blacks in the diaspora to seek immediate accommodation with imperialism. These intellectuals and elite stand as accomplished persons at the gates of imperialism, knocking at the door to be let in. They carry with them their certificates of praise for imperialism: *"Look at how much I have labored in your name; the people I have opposed in your name; the praises I have sung in your name, and the lengths to which I have gone in your name."*

These are offered as testimonials of their fidelity to imperialism. Some are admitted and elevated. And from these elevated positions they are paraded as evidence of a system that works for all. They are let loose to denounce all those who dare question the mercy and benevolence of imperialism. These activities, however well-funded and rewarded, cannot hide the insidious nature of imperialism. The sins of imperialism cannot be washed away by selectively anointing chosen few individuals as "leaders" of the oppressed groups.

Besides the seduction of wealth, power, and fame, there is also the added layer of cultural imperialism that spawn self-hatred, denial of self, and contempt for all that is inherently you. To such people, Trump spoke what they harbor in their chests, what they believe to be true and have been unable to utter in public. And so, although they will in public mutedly join the temporary noises of condemnation, they will remain forgiving; they will not see Trump's insults as a deal-breaker with him or what he stands for. And herein lies the problem.

What is mistakenly seen as perplexing and even confounding are reports of a few poor Africans on the continent who support Trump and hail him. We make a big mistake in imagining that an oppressed people automatically hate and resent their oppressors. Years of colonization and the force of power and cultural imperialism have been instrumental in implanting and sustaining admiration of the oppressor. Here you have some Africans, beyond the elite and the rich, and the rulers, cheering the racist and discriminatory practices of Trump. All those engaged in the quest for African revolution must not, must never, underestimate the resilient power of self-hatred that has completely seeped into our communities. We should never imagine that all of our people will, without adequate politicization, emerge committed to revolution, which includes the destruction of self-hatred and cultural imperialism. These sad and deplorable instances and exhibitions in themselves demonstrate that the problem of self-hatred (and confusion) among our people is more widespread than we may honestly wish to admit. It also demonstrates the flattening power of globalization and imperialism. The flooding of our airwaves and print and movies and other outlets of cultural imperialism have planted the seeds that venerate the imperial masters. What our people see is the power of imperialists, the land of grandeur and power and glamor. This is the land to be admired and the rulers to be admired, even if they preach hatred of us. No people can ever be free unless they liberate their mental enslavement and veneration of imperial masters. No people can advocate and strive for liberation if they announce and loudly proclaim their inferiority to the master.

The demystification of imperial power remains one of the most fundamental and essential assignments of radical revolutionary intellectuals. There can be no African revolution unless and until imperial power has been demystified. So long as imperial masters and what they represent are not demystified, there will be no revolution. If the masses remain mystified and continue to admire and venerate imperial leaders, institutions, etc., there can be no revolution. For we must agree that the power of Western cultural values over the African masses remains one of the most crucial weapons in its hold over us as a people and as societies. If our people come to imagine their future in the belly of imperialism, this leaves in place all imperial solutions, illusions, structures, and values.

This scattered admiration for Trump by a few Africans must readily show all radicals in our countries that the struggle is going to be long and complicated. The complexity of the revolution will involve not only the usual treacheries faced by all revolutionary movements but will also more prominently involve weaning sections of the local population from the suffocating power of imperialism. This reality introduces the corrupting force of what has come to be called, "common sense." The few African masses who have supported Trump can defend their actions by citing common sense. They know what they know due to common sense and common place information. These positions and even assertions bring to the fore two issues: how did they come to know what they think they know? Secondly, how do they know that what they know is true and valid? How people know, what they know, and more crucially, why people know what they believe they know, is a matter relevant to all efforts aimed at raising a people's consciousness. How did they come in contact with the information that they now claim as their own? And why do they defend such information? In the case of viewpoints emanating from imperial sources, why do the oppressed embrace utterances and positions that denigrate them? Are they aware that indeed they are being denigrated and despised even as they embrace imperial masters and their lauded spite? There can be no revolution on our continent until the revolutionary elite are able to break the connection and linkage of the African masses to this toxic information that under-develops us and promotes our self-hatred. This is a fundamental question.

Trump knew that few, if any, African governments would take great exception to these insults and utterances. A few isolated statements were issued, a few columns written, perhaps even speeches and lectures that received no coverage in the imperial press. These incoherent expressions of disappointment lacked the power and force to make the West know that disrespect for Africa has evident consequences.

There was no continental roar of anger and outrage. There were no consequences. African rulers were therefore quite happy and elated when Trump issued a perfunctory statement denying that he had meant to insult Africans. To these rulers, Trump's statement offered them a way out; a life raft that they could use to save themselves from the ridicule of their subjects. Now, back to business as usual.

Here, we see the dual confusion and illegitimacy of the African rulers. African rulers who do not really see themselves as Africans, and therefore as not affected by imperial slights, insults, and denigration. African rulers who have benefitted from and facilitated the exploitation and underdevelopment of Africa. African rulers who have betrayed the hopes and aspirations of Africans in the service of imperial plunder. The plunder that has led to insults like Trump's and many similar ones over the ages. Are they Africans?

On many levels, African rulers, the ruling elite in Africa, strutting across Africa on behalf of imperialism, have, with shameless relish, distanced themselves from the people they regard as their subjects, the people they oppress and exploit. They define themselves in foreign terms. Their real loyalty is to imperial masters. Their real respect is reserved for these external masters. They do not share a national purpose with the local populations, whom they regard and treat as their subjects. They do not believe in, and they have never pretended to believe in, the principle of equality of citizens. All of their economic, political, and social policies and programs reinforce again and again their deeply held belief in unequal citizenship.

And so, when Trump insults Africa and Africans, these rulers feel exempt. They are really not part of Africa. They see these insults as small matters, as just words with no real meaning or impact. They have always distanced themselves from Africa. They are the rich, opulent, and famous. In real terms, they have little in common with the poor, struggling, and loathsome masses, the real Africans, the true occupants of the "shit-hole countries." And herein lies the problem.

The Abaluyia of Kenya have, as part of their ethnic wisdom, a saying that can illuminate some of these weighty issues surrounding Trump's insults toward Africans. They say, "He who feeds you can insult your mother in your presence." All Africans, who adore their mothers, will immediately relate to the piercing power of the reality conveyed in this Abaluyia saying. Economic dependence creates a daunting disequilibrium in power relations. The dominated, the dependents, kowtow. They have no power; they lack the ability to forcefully react to correct this imbalance of power. Thus, there can be no corrective issued so long as the structures and systems that produce this imbalance remain in place. Economic dependence ensures that more insults and tirades against Africa and Africans will continue to flow in years ahead from the center of the empire. And, as has been in the past, appropriate biologically flavored rationalizations will be manufactured to offer high-sounding justifications for this imbalance, for this oppression and exploitation. Poverty, grafted onto policies of the treasonous neo-colonial rulers, has given rise to powerlessness. This powerlessness has, for the moment, denied Africans the power to resist and seek redress.

Theoretically, African governments and their African rulers are supposed to protect their citizens, which clearly includes their person, their safety, their health, their welfare, and, above all, their dignity as citizens of independent countries. We know that this has never been realized; or, rather, it has never been a prime objective of many of these neo-colonial rulers and the regimes over which they preside. These governments have, without shame or hesitation, ruled in the name of imperialism. Quite often these governments and the assembled ruling elite have behaved and acted as a foreign occupying power—undemocratic, and eager to plunder, oppress, and hurriedly exploit the local resources on behalf of the "Mother Country." They have not protected their citizens. If anything, they have consistently and systematically, terrorized, divided, and oppressed their citizens on behalf of imperialism.

It is therefore self-evident that, as a start, in order for Africans to feel respected and protected, they must exercise definite control over the disposal of the natural resources in their countries. This control must extend to the expenditure of the profits obtained from the sale of these natural resources. These resources constitute the collective birthright of all citizens. Since this is, technically, *their* wealth, it follows naturally that they should have a defining voice in how this wealth is disposed of. Their control over this wealth should be absolute. Trade must remain attached to verifiable respect and mutual benefit.

In those instances where local governments are despotic, corrupt, plunderous, and non-democratic, the actions of such governments should be seen as illegitimate. Such actions have no mandate from the citizens. Without mandate and legitimacy, these neo-colonial governments should not be allowed to have the dominant voice in the control and disposal of the country's national wealth. Wealth belongs to the people and must be accessed and utilized with their full, unequivocal consent. This fundamental change moves African countries and their peoples toward liberation.

As part of its international operations in the modern neocolonial period, imperialism comes to embrace the theoretical legal concept of national sovereignty of nations. Operationally, imperialism insists on the effective death of sovereignty. In order to have ready and accelerated access to the resources of the poor in the Global South, imperialism insists on dealing with the corrupt and inept comprador class. These thieves, this treasonous grouping, are paraded as the national authorities with the power to sign legally binding documents. The details of these complex documents are, in reality, irrelevant to the mission and strident objective of the comprador class. What they desire, what they salivate for, is their cut of the loot. They are robbers, whose basic interest is to get their small share of the loot. The people, the citizens, the owners of this wealth, are disregarded, never consulted. They are left to subsist in poverty and misery; conditions that are seized upon by imperialists and their lackeys as evidence of the natural ineptitude of Africans.

This diluted version of sovereignty will ensure that these countries in the Global South have no control over labor, especially the salaries, compensation, and working conditions of local workers. Nor will they have control over ownership of the natural resources, over pollution and environmental degradation, over repatriation of profits, or over the impact on local nascent industries and initiatives, etc. These, and related conditions, proclaim the power of imperialism and the fiction of sovereignty.

Trump and his cheerleaders, of course, expected Africans to forgive him, to provide him with immediate apologetic exoneration. Part of the uninterrupted privilege of imperialists is the power to insult the dominated people without apology. The oppressed and the exploited must forever endure and forgive. It is expected that the poor will promptly forgive the rich. The blood of the poor, the oppressed, the dominated, the despised, is expected to readily cleanse the sins of the rich and the powerful. By serving as permanent vehicles of forgiveness, the poor and the despised have over time come to occupy an indispensable role in the life cycle of the rich and the powerful: they have been assigned the deadly role of siphoning off the moral impurities of the system and its leaders. On an international level, we Africans, we people of African descent, have for the last five hundred years been shackled and coerced into performing this deadly role.

Part of our strides as Africans toward true liberation must involve the quick and forthright denunciation and abandonment of forgiveness; that is, abandonment of forgiveness toward our eternal oppressors and exploiters, toward those determined to humiliate us. We can, with abundance of evidence, affirm that we have done enough; we have forgiven enough; we have tolerated enough; we have endured enough; we have seen enough to know that our efforts have elicited derision, spite, humiliation, oppression, poverty, and unending repression. Now, it is time for the other side to also forgive, endure, and tolerate.

If indeed these are honorable traits, laudable qualities, why is it that we, as Africans and people of African descent, have carried the heaviest burden alone all these centuries? Time has come to put down the burden and let the other side carry it for a while. If these are the highest of ideals, then we should not hoard them, we should let the other side experience the joy of carrying them. What we know, what history teaches us, is that this painful suffocating burden will not be lowered from our shoulders unless and until we attain true liberation.

All those of our leaders who have insisted on us as Africans and people of African descent, being the eternal and permanent forgivers, have worked from the erroneous premise that salvation for us lies hidden in this racist, oppressive, and exploitative imperial system. They have also assumed that our salvation will be handed to us, if we behave well, by our imperial overlords. All available historical evidence demonstrates that this position is based on fantasy and delusion. We have behind us as part of our collective existence, five hundred years of pleading, petitioning, demonstrating, groveling, praying, agitating, and even proving ourselves. These, and related efforts, have in consequential terms, yielded minimal returns.

The problem facing the purveyors of the perfumed message of eternal forgiveness and endurance is that they have no power to alter our status in this imperial racist system. They cannot alter the structure, aims, and formulations of this system, which has racism and bigotry as key components of its tightly woven web. When do we attain *our* freedom, respect and liberation, *our* just and equitable share of the pie? And we must add here that we have, or are, responsible for the historical creation and then baking of this pie. Is this our eternal role—to merely admire from afar, even from our "shit hole countries," the consumption of this pie by our overlords? And where is the light, the credible verifiable light path, forward for us? Real light and not pious utterances that lull us to sleep only to be woken up to clean after the master.

On a fundamental level, we must not move away from continually asking why it has been necessary for us to agitate, petition, pray, etc. to prove our humanity and humanhood as a people. Why has our humanhood, our humanity, been in doubt, been a matter of debate and discussion? Why have we, as a people, been made to endure this humiliation on an international level? What is the rational basis of the relevant arguments? Can these arguments, in support of racism and bigotry, be justified?

Would those who have oppressed, exploited, despised, and humiliated us, those who have doubted our abilities, our mental capacities, our beauty and originality, would these people readily forgive if *they* were the victims of this persistent and vicious malice? Would *they* eternally forgive? How would they explain this eternal forgiveness to themselves? Of course, it is quite possible that some of them may, just to prolong a theoretical argument, state that indeed yes, they would forgive. But that is both irrelevant and offensive. For, after all, they have not been us, they are not us, they have not endured what we have endured over the ages. This may be an interesting, even invigorating, position to take in an abstract intellectual discussion. For us, it is a painful daily reality.

What we see in front us is that our oppressors and exploiters do not forgive. They are quick to resort to vengeful and spiteful retaliation. The practitioners of imperialism, racism, and bigotry do not endure; they do not forgive. They scan the local and the international, looking for vengeance. They do not forget the need for vengeance in order to reaffirm their prestige, authority, and unquestioned power. This is their basic definition, clothed in racism and bigotry.

GUNS AND VIOLENCE: CHILDREN AND STUDENTS AS VICTIMS IN THE USA

I

It happened again. It has happened again. There has been another mass shooting in a school in the USA. On February 14th, 2018, there was a horrific massacre of innocent students in Florida, specifically, at the Marjory Stoneman Douglas High School, in Parkland, Florida. About seventeen students were killed and many more wounded in a brazen attack on the school by a lone gunman. By any measure, this tragedy stands out as one of the worst in the world at the moment.

And, as expected here in the USA, there was a lot of hand wringing, inaudible sounds of mild evasive disapproval, pious expressions of vague solidarity with the families ("our hearts go out to them") in the coverage on TV stations spread across the country. And then the truly real inconsolable pain and anguish; devastating pictures of the anguished faces of distraught parents, teachers, and fellow students. This story, as is now customary, was in quick succession swept aside. There was another eye-catching tragedy to cover, and this one was brushed aside, effectively forgotten.

The USA is no longer surprised or even shaken by such tragedies. Since the massacre in Columbine High School in Colorado in 1999, there have been several equally shocking massacres in the USA—the Red Lake shootings in Minnesota, 2005; West Nickel Mines School in Pennsylvania, 2006; Virginia Tech University, 2007; Oikos University in California, 2012; Sandy Hook Elementary School, Connecticut, 2012; Umpqua Community College in Oregon, 2015; Marjory Stoneman Douglas High School in Parkland, Florida, 2018; and Santa Fe High School in Texas, 2018. Gun violence in general is common in the USA and now, regrettably, gun violence against students and young children is becoming commonplace.

It is this recurring attack upon students that exposes some of the nasty contradictions of this society, this country. From its inception, violence has been an integral defining entity of the American society, fabric, and essence. It is, if you like, deliberately woven into the American quilt of life and expectations. In the majority of the American experience, especially in its formative years, violence was the indispensable deliverer of riches, repeatedly employed to rob Native Americans of their land and resources (and then kill them); to institute and enforce slavery and other forms of unfree labor; to exploit labor and gender oppression; and to enforce draconian racist laws and a culture of racism, bigotry, and discrimination. The country has relied on violence to live and bask in the seductive lie of being a free society embracing freedom and justice for all.

Yet the incorporation of violence and guns as celebrated symbols of Americanness was bound to create unsettling contradictions. Guns were tolerated and even revered, even though they were instruments of robbery, enslavement, and then enforcement of rigid and unyielding discrimination. And in the hands of the police—mainly white police, guns continue to serve these historic roles by enforcing power, fear, oppression, and discrimination. But what happens when guns find outlets and expressions outside these traditional targets?

There can be little doubt that possession of guns in the modern USA is intricately linked to the tragedy of racism and the fear that inevitably issues from racial oppression and terror. The gun is seen by many whites (the majority of the gun owners) as their ultimate weapon of personal protection against an imagined and presumably impending racial uprising (or other forms of resistance and defiance) by African Americans in response to their hundreds of years of suffering indignities, oppression, discrimination, and exploitation. This fear—elemental and deep rooted, irrational yet blindingly real— defines and explains a series of social, economic and political problems in the USA. On some level, this fear defines the USA. This fear fuels gun sales and makes the USA a conglomerate of paranoia, tightly bottled anger, and irrationality. A country forever on edge, yet unable and unwilling to seriously revisit and engage its tortured past.

We should immediately remark that, as currently constituted, the USA has no credible answers or solutions to the gun problem. What is proposed, what has been routinely proposed, varies from doing nothing about expanding gun sales, to mild modifications in sales of guns (introducing slightly tighter controls), to background checks on would-be buyers, to locks on the guns or limits on the types of guns sold. Lately, this has also included attempts at profiling of potential buyers, denying people with mental health problems from buying or gaining access to guns, and, of course, secure storage of guns in homes. Yet again and again, all of these modifications or attempts to tackle the gun problem have proved hollow, evasive, and only marginally effective. What is not addressed, and what has been carefully avoided, is a robust serious national dialogue on the fundamental matter of guns and the USA. Why guns in the USA? Is this seen as a permanent feature of the country? Can this society envisage a country without guns?

Then there is the mythology of guns and safety. How can it be that the most armed country in the world is also very unsafe and irredeemably violent and insecure, especially to the youth? What discernible safety, for the individual and the society, have guns brought to the USA? Can this argument still be made with a straight face? Why does this argument continue to be considered rational, thus meriting allocation of national economic resources and political attention?

On top of all these, must be added the power of semi militarized police forces across the country, state armies, and federal armies. Many large universities now have robust and significant armed police forces. This is an armed country at every level. Yet, in spite of all these forces, guns, and more guns, the country remains stubbornly unsafe. Under these circumstances, fear, worry, alienation, paranoia, mistrust, anger, hostility, suspicion, depression, and stress-related illnesses abound and are disturbingly common. Research on, and even treatment of any one or all of these factors, falls into the realm of futility the moment the underlying causes are omitted, casually considered, or flippantly acknowledged.

A significant social and political drawback of imperialism is the utter unwillingness of the imperial powers to concede defeat and errors of judgement in their policy formulations (local and foreign). The powerful can never be wrong. The powerful, therefore, never apologize. The powerful have all the answers, even when this is patently untrue. And so, the USA has, with gusto, refused to revisit the social, economic, and political structures (and values) that produce this shameful violence. This country, which continues to deride non-white societies as primitive and barbaric on account of alleged violence in their societies, tolerates and indeed facilitates unparalleled and unsettling violence upon its citizens. This country has internalized the use of violence as its knee-jerk reaction to the settling of disputes, locally and overseas. You notice very quickly here that all roads pointing to the value of discussions, tolerance, and diplomacy are either dismissed or held suspect. They are seen as a sign of weakness. The powerful do not really negotiate. The powerful must dictate outcomes; just as they must dictate the terms of engagement in any conflict. There is a heightened need for a sort of national machismo in dealing with other countries. Force is power, and power is morality.

In its basic form, the USA foreign policy is the export of its domestic policy. The structure, inclinations, and prejudices so streamlined at home are exported overseas. They form the unshakeable foundation of the USA's engagement with foreign countries. All think tanks have, with minor variation, followed this scripture. The domestic structure has: sacred unquestioned elevation of business; dominant classes; emasculated working classes; oppressed and exploited workers; oppressed, exploited, and discriminated-against non-whites, especially African Americans; and harassed and exploited women. Thus, the world is viewed through this domestic prism. There are the good guys, those who support the USA imperial agenda, or have surrendered to this imperial hegemony. For the USA, its definition of diplomacy and world peace involves the surrender of countries and peoples to its imperial objectives. Any contrary ideology constitutes a veritable threat and must therefore be hunted down and eliminated. Naturally, in this arrangement, there can be no peace based on equality. Nothing bothers Americans as much as discussions about equality. Nothing so quickly propels Americans into a state of incomprehensible nervousness as discussions about equality.

In both domestic and foreign affairs, force remains the ultimate instrument of control. The only difference is the scale and varieties of violence unleashed. For overseas punitive expeditions, there are: Aircraft Carriers, the Air Force, and armies of all categories and gradations. The collective aim of this lethal and expensive firepower is to enforce the imperial agenda. The locals, usually non-white peoples, are expected to shake and surrender at the very mention of this immense force, the "lethal visit" from the Marines. The inestimable resources spent on assembling and maintaining this force is seen by the ruling classes as the best use of national intellectual and material wealth. This force patrols the outer edges of the empire and then, from time to time, enforces imperial power. And even when not engaged in actual war, this force has the added function of scaring, intimidating, frightening, and, yes, emasculating would-be enemies of the USA. When, after all of these efforts, the locals overseas do not signal surrender or obedience, the USA reverts to what it knows best: increase the volume, size, and quality of its lethal arsenal as the ultimate variable in all imperial encounters.

It is inevitable to think about this question of violence in the USA alongside the issue of ideology: the dominant national ideology. What has been avoided, what is never mentioned or seriously discussed, is the matter of the contradictions of capitalism and how these contradictions are stridently and forcefully linked to this shameful violence. Does this violence, sadly on the rise, not demonstrate the irrefutable evidence of the failure of capitalism? Can we avoid this question and continue to pretend that capitalism and the USA-led imperial system is infallible? There is now a rigidly and elaborately contrived devotion to this system, even as it shows on a daily basis that the roof is leaking and the foundation below is now so creaky and giving way.

Devotion to a creaky system, lumbering along, brings to memory the shape of the colonial system on the eve of the rise of mass nationalism in Africa and many parts of Asia. What we know is that the colonial office (of whatever imperial power) and most of the brain trust at the center of the empire were unwilling, and in some cases unable, to discuss the faults, weaknesses, and contradictions of the colonial system. Commissions were set up and studies undertaken to look into this or that problem, including massacres after some unspeakable imperial violence against the colonized. At best, these efforts resulted in minor modifications of policy, while leaving the foundation and fabric of the system undisturbed. This system was viewed, and publicized, by the imperial powers as forward looking and almost infallible, except for minor operational details that required periodic adjustments. All the writings, all the learned treatises, all the celebrated commentaries about this system were in the end fraudulent escapades and an expensive waste of resources. A system burdened by its own contradictions has rarely, if at all, provided answers to its own mistakes while remaining intact.

Going back to the question of ideology, let us imagine for a moment that this haunting and shameful scale of violence were occurring in the Soviet Union during the Cold War. Let us imagine that young Soviet men (mainly) were shooting and killing other young people in schools or committing this unspeakable violence. And that this had become a national crisis. Let us also imagine that the Soviet Union was generally seen as a violent society with a long -troubled history of widespread inequality, social injustice, racial discrimination, and bigotry. And let us imagine that there were no official efforts to address these problems earnestly and aggressively. Let us imagine all these. What would have been the response of the West, and especially the USA? Would any response and critique have failed to link all of these issues to the ideological question? Would any response from the West ever escape mentioning that these social problems and maladies are directly linked to the failure of communism?

On TV screens, in elaborate published commentaries, journals, and then at well-funded conferences, we would see Western experts, on the Soviet Union, Russia, describing and explaining the failures of communism and how these inherent and operational defects account for the violence engulfing the Soviet society.

But now, with regard to capitalism and violence, US (Western) voices are silent on the question of ideology. The critiques can go only so far. They stop far short of dissecting and then presenting to the public the rotten inner contents of capitalism and imperialism and how these contradictions have to be accounted for in order to both explain this violence and find credible solutions.

What makes this problem of guns and violence most unsettling for the ruling classes in the USA is that it cannot be blamed on some ill-meaning foreigners, communists, or revolutionaries from the Global South or an assortment of foreign militants. It is most American. It is most domestic. And here lies the problem. We know that if these many shooters had been foreigners espousing some ideology of sorts, Marines would have been hastily dispatched to the supposed home country of the culprits. Disproportionate revenge would have been summarily inflicted on those societies with frenetic vigor. The USA is eager, very eager, to severely punish foreigners and minorities for these acts of violence. But it lacks the purpose, energy, and machismo to defend its own children.

The adults in power look at these children as dispensable casualties in the struggle (and war) to maintain and reinforce the system of sectional privileges, attention, and oppression. What happened to all the voluble declarations about defending the family and the children? Can the US government and its several agencies collectively defend its citizens and its children from *internal* violence? Can American children be provided with a safe physical and emotional environment in which to grow and prosper? And can this be undertaken and achieved under the current capitalist and imperial system?

II

Impatient with ineffective and, frankly, nonexistent positive government response after the massacre in Parkland, Florida, thousands of students (mainly high school students) resolved to rouse their leaders into action by undertaking massive mobilization against gun violence. Several members of the dominant institutions, especially the National Rifle Association (NRA), after a brief moment of silence on the matter, voiced opposition to these student protests. The NRA, like other dominant social institutions, saw the inevitable, invisible hand of communists, radical teachers, politicians, etc., behind these protests. These students were seen as immature, irresponsible, ungrateful spoiled brats, daring to oppose the holy script of the American way, by which the ruling elite means capitalism and imperialism and their encasing values.

These protests provide clear evidence of massive yet uncoordinated resistance against guns and gun violence in the country. They are a vivid example of spontaneous resistance. Yet the students will quickly find that spontaneous resistance, however brave and spirited, is not enough. There is something to be admired about spontaneity and unplanned activism born out of rage and immediate anger. History, however, teaches us that spontaneity alone cannot lead to revolutionary and consequential change. Groups and individuals involved in the initial upsurge of resistance tend to lose interest after a while and readily resume their life patterns and occupations from before the resistance. Tempers calm down and ancient worries reappear and consume efforts and attention. The ruling classes have traditionally counted on this factor to sap the energy out of such resistance, alongside deploying multiple intelligence and security forces to combat any semblance of sustained coordination.

There is, therefore, a crucial and inescapable need for organization, for systematic and deliberate organization. Such organization will ensure that these powerful energies, contained in the initial fury, are not wasted and abandoned. Organization will provide focus, refine the arguments, and seek to maintain momentum. Organization will adjust strategies depending on changing events and prevailing local and national circumstances.

On one level, it can be argued that this matter of guns and gun violence, can easily be resolved through established national political institutions: through elections, amending the constitution, or even through the judiciary. But why has this not happened? Why have the established institutions and structures failed to resolve this urgent national problem?

Theoreticians of Western Liberal Democracy have presumed the existence of an active and informed electorate. An informed, engaged, and independent-thinking electorate. They have presumed that decisions so made by the electorate represent informed free will. We know that this is not true. The flooding of newsprint, then airwaves, and now social multi-media outlets with enormous erroneous and false advertisements mock the very existence of the power of free will in the making of these crucial decisions. Money buys political power. Money retains power. Thus, wealth equals power and seeks to employ power to enhance wealth and all the explicit and implicit advantages that flow from wealth.

The presumption that the electorate scrutinizes and debates all issues and votes out of free informed will is an advantageous façade erected and maintained by the wealthy in order to bestow a modicum of legitimacy on the creaky, corrupt system. The example of the exercise of democracy in the West has therefore been disconcerting. It starts with hiding the truth from the electorate. It starts with looking down on the electorate and thus dismissing out of hand whatever they think. It starts with diluting and simplifying issues and ideas to mere sound bites. It starts with playing up the toxins of race, bigotry, discrimination, and loathing of foreigners. It starts with scaring the electorate into submission. It starts with erecting almost impenetrable walls of separation between the oppressed peoples and the incisive eye -opening analyses of social, political, and economic problems confronting them. It avoids dissemination of true verifiable information.

The success of the ruling classes in the West has partly been dependent upon their ability to popularize and then keep in place the mythology that revolution, and the quest for revolutionary change in the status quo, is anti-West, anti-society, anti-common sense, even maybe treasonous; that to be Western, to be a true American, one has to abhor and be resistant to any and all revolutionary change. In this way, the current capitalist oppressive system, characterized by exploitation, oppression, racism, and discrimination, constitutes the West that must be venerated. No class in the West is immune from this debilitating and paralyzing outlook. This ideological paralysis is most evident among the educated elite, the progressives, and then the middling classes. They cannot imagine living in a world in which the West is not at the helm. To them, normal is a world dominated by Western values, Western definitions of concepts, and Western power and institutions. And, more fundamentally, they accept (although not so loudly in the current period) that the West is superior to the rest of the world.

One of the enduring, signature, paralyzing impacts of capitalism in the USA (and the West in general) has been to make the populations eternally afraid. These are terrified people, yet almost religious in their awe of wealth, glamor, power, and privilege—beaten down, so terrified, so controlled, so manipulated, so atomized, so very individualistic, so suspicious of social movements. This obedience, which appears on stage as individualism, ensures that the ruling classes are not really worried at the moment about the revolutionary potential of the working class, the poor, the unemployed, the petit bourgeoisie, those existing on the fringe of society. From time to time there will be discontent. But the ruling classes, through tested and vibrant networks of spies and counterspies, quickly spring into action to punish would-be mobilizers. This means that revolutionary messages, including those on guns and violence, have continually been denied a home and reception in the working class, and even among the poor.

As a result, there is a pervasive sense of powerlessness of the people vis-à-vis the ruling classes. It is almost as if there is now in the USA (and the West) an established permanent ruling elite, a sort of powerful nobility without the feudal titles. The poison of the rationalization of the status quo, which constitutes the accepted justifications for the status quo, have sunk so deep in the political and mental reflexes of the majority of the people. Their instinct is to obey, to serve, to accept the reality and power of their status so as to survive, and then to seek for diversions from their inner sorrow and powerlessness. This inner sorrow, like volcanic magma, occasionally erupts with uncontrollable violence.

The possession of guns is tolerated so long as it is understood that these guns are supposed to be aimed at fellow workers, and the fellow poor, preferably from the dominated groups. And the ruling classes know that this will always be the case. It will always be this way. No guns in the hands of workers or the oppressed groups will be allowed to invade the protected neighborhoods of the ruling classes and threaten their lives and status. A concerted invasion of the enclaves of the rich and powerful would have to be the result of some recognizable political awakening and consciousness. The rich and the ruling classes will never allow this awakening to occur and survive.

Within the current political alignment in the USA, these students can be forgiven for imagining and then hoping that the Democratic Party could be their natural ally on this question of guns and violence in schools. These students could, understandably, look to the Democratic Party for consolation and maybe even an active embrace of their aims. Yet this is unlikely to be true. The Democratic Party, it turns out, is not as anti-gun and anti-violence as its rhetoric may superficially suggest. On this question of guns and violence, as with many other crucial issues, the Democratic Party has a variety of positions and answers.

The many groupings that fall under the general umbrella of the Democratic Party lack unity of purpose and, in many cases, coherence. There is no agreement as to what constitutes the key problems ailing the country, and especially its most vulnerable citizens. As a result, there is no united narrative, except for vague and wobbly inclination(s) toward some notion of social justice. And even with this notion, there is a deliberate vagueness, a lack of credible definition. This makes it difficult to measure progress toward the desired goal. The several ideological stirrings, trends, dispositions, tendencies in the party have essentially led to a perennially hobbled party, unable to act with precision and decisiveness on key national issues. And above all, there is the Party's untenable thesis that equality, social justice, fairness, and an end to racism can all be attained within the framework of the current capitalist and imperial system; that racism, bigotry, sexism, oppression, and exploitation, can be ended within this capitalist imperial system.

And so, there is a call for an end to some runaway practice of injustice, instituting this and that control over some unacceptable social practice, increased funding for some program geared for the poor, curtailing police brutality, etc. In other words, the Democratic Party looks at its duty and obligation as being essentially the trimming off of the noxious excesses in the system, as that of a sort of studious and informed gardener. And, that such an exercise will lead to the good society. Reform the system and it will deliver goodness, social justice, and prosperity for all. But can this ever occur? Why has the Democratic Party failed to deliver on the question of guns and violence?

Democratic Party politicians appear timid, afraid, and insecure. They appear as if they are occupants of a house that does not belong to them, leasing the house under strict conditions until the owners return from their vacation. They cannot, therefore, dare tinker with the shape of the house or even attempt any consequential modifications. Democratic Party politicians, in demeanor and positions held, appear as if they feel compelled to reassure the country (especially the radical Right) that they mean no harm to the system and to conservatives and their values. If anything, they end up overreaching in seeking for collaboration with the radical Right and the conservatives. The price is usually too steep, so steep as to negate all efforts aimed at advancing the Democratic Party agenda and moving toward an egalitarian society. This includes the search for solutions to the gun problem.

The radical Right and the conservatives always count on this endemic and perennial insecurity of the Democrats. They can count on the Democrats jumping every time someone doubts their devotion to the industrial-military complex. And in this way, this money-making (and wasteful) complex continues to reap unchecked profits even under the Democrats. Also, Democrats work from conclusions evident in the analyses of the radical Right and the conservatives about the poor, especially on social welfare. Tough on crime, tough on everything dealing with the poor. But not tough on corporate thievery and financial crimes. But not tough on income inequality. But not tough on police violence against the poor and the oppressed, especially African Americans. But not tough on racism. But not tough on curbing and eliminating violence in schools and providing a credible formula for protecting children and students in their schools. But not tough on corporate environmental crimes. But not tough on provision of living wages for the working class. In this way, therefore, there exists, in reality, minute differences between the Republican Party and the Democratic Party. The Republicans are avowedly racist, sexist, and enthusiastically imperialist; and they oppress and exploit openly without apology. Democrats construct an unwieldy narrative to explain their limited consequence. This narrative is full of confusion, contradictions, and reversals. In the end, nothing really changes. This, unfortunately, incudes the much-needed consequential action on guns and gun violence.

On another level, it can be argued that these students—plus the routinely excluded women and the poor—who have staged their own demonstrations in opposition to official policies, are in essence fighting for their liberation. Their marches are expressions of disapproval. They do not march because they are happy with the system, this system that oppresses and exploits them and does not care for them. These are protests of resistance to and not of approval of the system in power. To be sure, the protests are several and diverse and disparate, but they signal a tenable and persistent desperation from below.

These protests are routinely ignored, and their consequence or significance dismissed. However massive, these protests are viewed as temporary outbursts by idle excitable non- consequential mobs. The media joins in this crusade of dismissiveness. The demonstrations are covered as spectacle, with no discernible consequence for the republic and its steady institutions and values. But this same media and a myriad of experts will eagerly seize on incidents of protests and demonstrations in countries in the Global South (or ideological enemies of the West) as evidence of political discontent in those countries. Why this difference in coverage, analysis, and consideration? In the USA, these massive demonstrations are clothed in nothingness. Their power is dismissed. One of the disturbing aspects of the US ruling classes is their lack of respect for the citizens on a daily basis.

And yet these protests and demonstrations by students should be a source of worry to the ruling elite, for different reasons. We know that political and economic systems fall when they fail to reproduce themselves in the young, when their values and prejudices fail to be reproduced in their young. It has been taken for granted that the American capitalist and imperial system (with all of its burdens) will be eternally reproduced in the young.

But is this necessarily true in the years ahead?

ON HUNTING BLACKS

I

You start, in the USA, by immediately acknowledging that dotted across the country are several white supremacy groups. They vary in size and notoriety from the traditional KKK (Ku Klux Klan) to Neo-Nazis, White Power Skinheads, Oath Keepers, Proud Boys, Militias, etc. All of these groups advocate white power supremacy. They are racist hate groups. Their rationale for existence is to reinforce and expand uncontested white supremacy—the cherished old system of dominant and unbending white dictatorship—and, therefore, to subject nonwhite groups, especially African Americans, Latinos, people of Asian descent, and Jews, to brutality, harassment, oppression, humiliation, and, of course, exploitation. The hatreds that pervade the country, that create the searing contradictions of the USA, are all related to white supremacy. All these white supremacy groups cause fear, terror, and then violence. Established laws, social and political structures, and the overall structural domination are all aimed toward affirming white supremacy. We need to bear this in mind as we encounter the polished and contradictory condemnation of white supremacy groups in the media; this is the media traditionally identified as "mainstream" in the country. Immovable contradictions in the media in areas of racism, exploitation, oppression, and discrimination demonstrate that it is folly to imagine that there is a sea of difference between the supporters of traditional institutional structures of white supremacy and hate-filled non-traditional groups. The reality is that such claims of difference are insincere in substance and overall national impact.

To this must be added the need to analyze the justification traditionally embraced, and forcibly propagated, by these white racist groups for their shameful and obnoxious actions of violence, harassment, and intimidation. These groups have held onto the claim that they, and their white brethren, and only they own the country. That this country is for whites, and therefore non-whites are imposters, foreigners, illegal—squatters, undesirable, and not supposed to be here. Length of residence in the country is irrelevant. No matter how recent the arrival, if you are white you move to the privileged head of the line and rightfully lay claim to the country; it is yours. But it does not, and cannot, and should not, and will not, belong to non-whites irrespective of length of stay and existence in the USA. This will always be "the white man's country." It cannot belong to nonwhites even if history unequivocally shows that it is non-whites who are responsible for building the country, for developing the country. The country will forever be classified and defined as white, while history stubbornly shows that white homicidal violence is responsible for nearly annihilating the populations of the true (original) owners of this country. Here we are talking of the near annihilation of Native Americans. Violence by white supremacists is embraced and perpetrated in keeping with past practices; practices from a time when white violence was used to rob and kill, to enforce and perpetuate slavery and then continued racial discrimination; and create a society that has embraced two contradictory positions: white supremacy under the cover of an unresolved claim to freedom. This is how we follow the path that points us to yet another murder of an African American by whites in the USA.

On February 23rd, 2020, Ahmadu Arbery, a 25-year-old African American man, was pursued and then killed by two white men, father and son. Arbery was killed after being hunted by Travis McMichael and his father Gregory McMichael, who were armed with guns and in a truck, which they used to track Arbery as he jogged in Glyn County, in Georgia. The two white men had decided to hunt down Arbery because they deemed him suspect, in the wrong place, by which this means he was in an area effectively designated as white and opposed to the presence of African Americans. The story of this killing became widely known across the country and beyond, once the video surfaced showing moments of confrontation and then the shooting of Arbery by Travis Michael. It is useful to remark here that George McMichael is a former police officer, retired in 2019 in Georgia.

These shootings, these killings by whites murdering blacks, have become so routine in this country. Those of very recent memory include: Trevon Martin (Sanford, Florida, 2012); Eric Garner (Staten Island,

New York, 2014); Michael Brown (Ferguson, Missouri, 2014); Akai Gurley (Brooklyn, New York, 2014); Aura Rosser (Ann Arbor, Michigan, 2014); Tamir Rice (Cleveland, Ohio, 2014); Freddie Grey (Baltimore, Maryland, 2015); Janisha Fonville (Charlotte, NC, 2015); Michelle Cusseaux (Phoenix, Arizona, 2015); Alton Sterling (Baton Rouge, Louisiana, 2016); Philando Castille (Falcon Heights, Minnesota, 2016); Jean Botham (Dallas, Texas, 2018); Stephon Clark (Sacramento, California, 2018); Breonna Taylor (Louisville, Kentucky, 2020); George Floyd (Minneapolis, Minnesota, 2020); Rayshard Brooks (Atlanta, Georgia, 2020); and Daniel Prude (Rochester, New York, 2020).

All of these murders (and more), have to be seen as an exercise in open season on black people. That, in fact, white people hunt black people in this country. That they look at black people as target; that is, a target to be hunted and killed. And that this killing is, in itself, done to reinforce white power. This country has looked at the killing of black people as legitimate and sanctioned. Nor can we forget that for a long time there was no prosecution of any kind to any white man who shot, lynched, or beat to death a black person, especially during slavery, and largely during Jim Crow. This was seen as justified killing. The possession of guns, the use of lethal force, and the constant display of guns in public by white people, especially white men, serves one simple purpose: to hold this system of racial oppression and privilege in place. Hence, the best way of ensuring that this system is kept in place is to continually frighten, harass, and intimidate black people. From the inception of this country as one of white supremacy, fear has been an integral part of racial oppression. Force to frighten the oppressed and exploited, to deter any resistance from the dominated people. Kill in the open, lynch in the open, in order to frighten, to deter. A frightened, oppressed people, routinely murdered, come to focus on survival; they lack the capacity to immediately resist, overthrow. They learn to defer for personal and family survival; and they have to know when to salute, avoid confrontation. Internally, they endure seething anger and frustration, which humiliate and kill them. To survive they have to contort and discipline their bodies, facial muscles, tone of voice, and eye movements into a display of obedience and surrender as desired by the master. This is humiliation that is woven into the social structure, expectation, and tradition.

Those white men (mainly) who kill African Americans do expect the rest of the white society to hail them, to laud them, for a job well done. For, after all, how can they be wrong when they have rendered such warrior service to the race? They expect the white society to be grateful, to feel secure because, in killing, they have frightened black people and therefore reaffirmed the power and structure of the system. It is an error to dismiss this factor that hovers over the aims and overall intent of white supremacists. In the past, there was outright acquittal; now there is no real prosecution, just perfunctory prosecution that leads to acquittal since no evidence is available or determined. The legal system continues to acquit the killers and condemn the victims. This is the weight of the past, a weight that the society has embraced. These constant killings explain the sale of guns and the rationale that routinely steps to the podium to provide justification.

And here lie the knotted and insurmountable contradictions in the USA. For, on one hand, this society wishes to project itself, to advertise itself, as a society ruled by law, and therefore, law abiding. This is the deeply held mythology that propels this society forward. On the other hand, there is the ever-present stubborn reality that enables, then sanctions, this society to condone violation of any laws when this is in the interest of controlling black people and limiting their growth and development. At such moments, laws do not count; they can be by-passed and explained away through creative innovation and manipulation and evasiveness of the law. Here, law is sidelined, it becomes an instrument to enforce oppression, bigotry, racism, and exploitation. Political, social, and economic power determine the definition and meaning of law. It is quick to see that law ceases to have power and meaning whenever black people have to be controlled, frightened, and scared into compliance and obedience. Law does not erase the hunting of black people by whites. And since white people do not in any way look at black people as real people, as people, as equals, this hunting is neither a new development nor a unique inexplicable surprise. It follows the meaning, definition, and intent of racism that promotes and celebrates dehumanization of all those deemed to be inferior to the superior master race. Hunting blacks becomes the fullest expression of this long-standing dehumanization of black people for hundreds of years, a dehumanization that denies equality of humanity.

On some very fundamental level, therefore, the humiliation and then murder of George Floyd must be seen as falling within the long-established practice of both hunting blacks and denying their humanity. On March 25th, 2020, George Floyd, an African American man, was killed in Minneapolis, Minnesota. He had been arrested by the local police, having been accused of "allegedly passing a counterfeit $20 bill in Minneapolis." At the point of his arrest, this time within the close eye-view of many witnesses with cell-phone cameras, especially Darnella Frazier, a white police officer proceeded to kneel on Floyd's neck for what seemed like an eternity; close to nine minutes. This resulted in Floyd's death even as he had implored the police officer to stop kneeling on his neck since he could not breathe. He said this again and again, as Derek Chauvin, the police officer, as recorded by Darnella Frazier, kept kneeling on his neck, unconcerned, unmoved. A deliberate and vile racist death crime that seemed not to bother the several police officers who watched Floyd choke to death. From afar and from up-close, African Americans watched another black person dying at the hands and feet of a white man in the open, without restraint. This death reaffirmed that indeed, as African Americans, we are a hunted people and any one of us can be isolated for violence and vengeance at any time. Living is, for us, a deliberate defiance of this manhunting by whites. African Americans have lived and survived in spite of fear; gained aspects of growth in spite of fear; they have lived as a people in spite of fear; they have lived as a people eager to attain some development and even life itself, before they encounter violence and even death at the hands of whites and the system that they control and maintain.

Floyd's death struck a coiled nerve among the African Americans, initially in Minneapolis and then around the country and beyond. They could see that Chauvin seemed unconcerned, not afraid, defiant without any hint of remorse. This image brought to the surface the many past and recent killings of African Americans at the hands of whites, including white police. Here they were as a people once again under perennial siege from white supremacy. And this time, white supremacy groups had come out in the open to mingle with their mainstream white defenders, finding in Trump a champion who openly embraced them and their vision. Emanating from several media outlets and from the mouth of Trump himself, were what the African Americans felt was unchecked white supremacy: that the walls of this world, of this moment, were deliberately cutting off any exits toward any form of possible moderation. What they saw was an unchecked escalation of violence, venom, and a march toward triumphant supremacy, with no more need for code words or euphemisms. Nor could they forget the strutting of whites and whiteness across the land, the unhindered bellowing of the racists instigated and then protected by Trump. All of these painful memories led to the nerve being struck at this moment. And to this must be added the continued excessive death, the disproportionate death, of African Americans due to the coronavirus. This virus continued to kill more African Americans than whites, and this regrettable outcome is the result of poverty that remains steeped in pre-existing endless racism. Poverty that is result of exploitation and racism.

The outburst of anger over Floyd's murder was the outrage that emerges from spontaneity. But as the anger grew, it widened into pre-existing poverty, oppression, and, of course, racism. Floyd's murder opened a flood gate of endemic, deep-rooted social injustice that has always remained based on racial oppression and economic exploitation. While so many ideas were floated to explain the anger and the outrage, it was evident that this was resistance against the USA system by the poor, the marginalized, the oppressed, the neglected, those on the margins of the society. The system itself was exposed, again. The men and women on the move in resistance had endured the arrogance and cruelty of the rich, of those who own the society. This resistance also demonstrated that in fact the poor have never accepted the basis of the status quo: the USA system. They have refused to accept this status as legitimate and permanent. Inside those heavy hearts that carry the labor of the rich and smile in front of the rich, is boiling anger that they hold down like magma below the surface in order to survive. In these temporary moments of free expression of what lies in their hearts, it was easy to see this anger, this rage against the system that relies on race, racism, sexism, poverty, exploitation, and oppression.

As the resistance took hold across the country, there were the constant questions about the fact of police brutality that goes unchecked. This brutality has, in essence, put the country under permanent military siege. This siege both rewards and continually confuses this society, whose people are instructed to recite on command that, indeed, "this is the greatest country in the world." This theory, which is really anxiety, forbids the people from challenging the meaning of the country, the practical meaning of this theory. If indeed this is the greatest country in the world, then all that is required, the only work, the only effort, is to accede and defend. To challenge the theory that is used to govern the country is to be held suspect, and therefore dismissed, avoided, and even punished. Loyalty forbids excessive reflection on the historical impact of this theory. The loud voices in the media, academy, political structure, and religions aggressively asserting the uniqueness of the country, are really meant to repress and silence any expansive and historical discussion on the origin, formation, and shaping of the country. What is valued, what is treasured, is to proclaim and loudly re-affirm the greatness of the country that stands above all others, and that this uniqueness has remained indifferent to history. This is the meaning of the cherished scholarship that, in reality, perpetuates racism, poverty, bigotry, and social injustice. This resistance, in response to the murder of Floyd, for a moment forced the country and its population to confront its past. They had to face a few of the details that have been sidestepped, overlooked, under-valued, denied, and rejected.

In the rallies, people pushed forward, agitated, and furious. In anger, they looked united. A rather unique and rare exhibition of group work in a country that is premised on individualism. In history, especially Western historical research and analysis, special attention has been paid to non-emotional facts, meaning, and formulation. To be emotional, to be roundly angry, is to be declared non-rational, and certainly those deemed as non-rational cannot bear merit or seriousness of consideration.

Thus, those who evince emotion, anger, and agitation have no credibility on the issues under discussion or consideration. You must be non -emotional, avoiding agitation, in order to be rational and admitted for possible consideration. Therefore, there can be no credibility or validity attached to fury, anger, and agitation. But we know that this is not true. History, it turns out, cannot escape from emotion and anger. There is no history without emotion, anger, activism, and forthright determination. There can be no history without emotion, anger, and focus. Thus, to downplay emotions—or even to dismiss them—in historical analysis, is to deny the existence and value of those many people who risked everything, believing in their grievances, focus, and aims.

In the rallies around the country, emotion, rage, and anger were infused with grievances. There was focus on agitation over poverty, social injustice, brutality, neglect, and the humiliation imposed repeatedly on the oppressed. It would be difficult to calmly separate these factors. By placing what is considered rationality over emotion, we invalidate the pain and humiliation that repeatedly hurt the oppressed and the exploited. People can, and do, express both emotional anger at and expression of their grievances. The oppressed are instructed to express their pain calmly; distant and unemotional. They may be listened to—or rather, their complaints may be filed in the drawer of the oppressors—if the poor wretched people can educate themselves to speak calmly, with respect, and wait patiently for responses from the master. The filed complaints are thrown away and forgotten, never to be engaged again.

The master provides answers and desirable outcomes considered acceptable, which means outcomes that do not change the system and the power of the master. Rational analysis and answers sanctioned and endorsed by the master effectively push from the table complaints and grievances from the oppressed. The power of the master to exercise control over historical events and factors dominates what can and what cannot be brought to the table for consideration.

What transpired was a knee-jerk reaction from the defenders of the system, who saw the barbarians at the gates. Here were the riff-raffs at the gates, clowning in the streets in the name of resistance. How dare they? And what do they know? These were the margins of society making ill-advised pronouncements on issues and matters that they can never understand. They must be stopped. And this can be done by springing into action and mobilizing the hidden and open powers of the system. The rich, the powerful, and the owners of the country do not tolerate any form of struggle against their system. To allow resistance to fester is to subject the system to critiques that provide examples of its horrors, brutality, and indifference. Rallies and resistance could not be tolerated and allowed to venture beyond acceptable fashions, ideas, and versions. By lambasting the rallies as unruly and too radical, the rich and the powerful used this moment to reaffirm and reinforce the eternal values of capitalism and imperialism. All those involved in the rallies had to remain true to the political, economic, and social values of the USA. Thus, the rallies must end up where they started, reaffirming the structure and history of the USA, the largely unaltered racist system of capitalism and imperialism.

Rallies and resistance came to focus on statues in the country as symbols of oppression and humiliation. Loud voices agitated for the statues of the master to be torn down and removed from public view. The country was being forced to encounter largely uncomfortable and even intolerable definitions of history and historical memory. These are definitions that have been left untouched, with no elaborate disclosure. Statues of the master have, over the years, been untouchable, too important to be subjected to justification. And this effortless existence of statues, in itself, affirms the power of the powerful. In not challenging, the oppressed acquiesce in their own powerlessness and the deliberately enforced narrative of the past. This is held as the true identity of the country. The multiple existence of statues is hence political and social. All those conservatives and white supremacists who furiously came out in support of statues spoke in defense of the national culture and history, *their* history. The statues are valid on account of longevity; they should be left untouched, for they have stood untouched for a long time. Longevity is justification, validity, and legitimacy. But why were the statues erected and venerated?

The fear attached to the dismantling of some of the prominent statues raised alarm bells in the hearts of the rich and the powerful and the supremacists; that the fall of the statues signaled open and daring challenge to the well-choreographed theories that affirm and justify the system and its exploitation and brutality. Trump argued that old statues should be left untouched for they represent the country's history. The purpose of his remarks was to reenergize his base of political support, composed of right-wing whites who raged in anger as the rallies expanded across the country. The stated and unstated aim and impact of Trump's rumblings was clear: dismiss and deride the value of African Americans to the country's history and its achievements. African Americans are erased and, in doing so, slavery, racism and oppression are equally erased. This consistent hold onto "history of the past" by white supremacists, and by the owners of the country, reiterates the importance of racism and capitalism. Statues are a constant reminder of the power of the past and the present, and constant adherence to racism and brutality.

II

The rising tide of rallies created some largely unspoken and not overtly articulated ideological questions. Can we have social justice while endorsing capitalism and, therefore, racism? What will be the meaning and structure and expanse of social justice if it supposedly walks alongside capitalism? These questions become even more troubling when the liberal mainstream media is brought in to adjudicate over the rallies. For a while, the coverage was spectacle and also wonderful for profits at a time when the coronavirus played havoc on several sections of the capitalist enterprise. But you immediately started to see the end of the line for the media. If some of the rallies become identified as being against or at least critical of the capitalist system, then the temporary shaking of hands ceases to exist; they evaporate, and the new forthrightness of opposition is set in motion. The centerpiece of the media is to cheer the existence and triumph of capitalism and, of course, imperialism. The media cannot cheer the rallies if they turn the corner and point the finger at corruption, and racism and, of course, capitalism.

This reality will once again bring this inherent contradiction to the fore for the elite and educated African Americans; for those who have embraced the power of capitalism and have slept, sometimes in agony, over its oppression and humiliation of African Americans. On many occasions, they have been called upon to stand up and defend capitalism even as it has denigrated,

humiliated, oppressed, and exploited African Americans. How do they respond to those voices in the rallies speaking earnestly against capitalism? Is the path forward to merely stand aside and then write long narratives while still endorsing capitalism? Is the pathway to progress, liberty, end of racism, all firmly located in capitalism? The fundamental objective remains to be the meaning of social justice and the end of racism. On this issue, it can be agreed that rallies will separate and disintegrate once this objective ceases to be sheer vague pronouncements on a system created to uphold and advance capitalism and racism.

These questions will also come to apply to the rallies as they move into the future. For we should immediately state that not all those moving into the rallies oppose capitalism. A number of them will restate their compliance with the USA in its current structure: as capitalist, sacrosanct, and therefore above any form of reproach. If capitalism stands above reproach, then surely racism remains intact.

The immediate anger and sets of grievances have correctly been directed toward the brutality of the police and the obvious discrimination against the African Americans. This carries with it a multitude of complex problems that cannot be resolved without bringing into focus the foundational structure of the country. Can non-discrimination exist independent of poverty and employment? Can non-discrimination exist independent of housing, education, income, and power? To be sure, in the immediate moment, the power of the police can be restrained and guided. But is this enough? And indeed, can the power of the police be restrained independent of the social structure? What kind of restraint will be tolerated and accepted? Who will enforce this restraint? What will happen when the scales of the rallies wind down and the force of their charge ceases to be easily visible? How will rallies find a home in the social structure?

The Black Lives Matter movement (BLM) was the clarion call of the rallies spread across the country and in many parts of the world, including parts of the European Union. BLM was founded in 2012 by three African American women activists: Patrisse Cullors, Alicia Garza, and Opal Tometi, largely in response to the murder of Trayvon Martin, in Florida. At the fundamental level, this became an avid outcry at all the brutality summed up in the murder of Floyd. This later migrated into resistance against widespread racism, brutality, and bigotry, principally against black people. Also included was gender discrimination against LGBTQ people.

BLM has, in turn, forced the USA to pay attention to the racist thuggery and bigotry that it has repeatedly refused to acknowledge. On this fact, and many related to this moment, we have to agree that indeed BLM has been an extraordinary achievement, a courageous call to arms.

Overseas, BLM expanded its reach to include heated discussions about the African slave trade and slavery and colonialism. King Leopold's statue in Belgium was torn down. In the UK, the 17th-century slave trader, Edward Colston, was toppled in Bristol. Discussions about Winston Churchill emerged even as the rooted establishment rose to defend him. It was instructive to read about the loud defense of Churchill by the rooted and powerful establishment, and especially by scholars in the UK and beyond: yes, he held racist beliefs, he was an avid imperialist, but this was in keeping with the ideas and opinions of his day; and above all, he saved Britain from Hitler and the Nazis. Whatever his mistakes may be, he saved Britain and therefore his statue has to be left standing. He is simply too important for Britain and for its historical definition and claim to imperial glory. In other words, people can be forgiven in spite of their egregious mistakes so long as they are British and are from the West; so long as they are champions of the West and, of course, defenders of imperialism.

The West is unforgiving whenever radical nationalists, let alone revolutionaries, are mentioned and brought up for discussion. They are never forgiven. Their past is doused in venom and anger. And, of course, they have no positive attributes to uphold. Their actions and ideologies are inevitably maligned and lambasted.

These various condemnations are then put in well-knit books and shipped overseas for study by the oppressed. In the West, the several well-knit books receive expansive exposure to become the mainstream narratives. In turn, they are infused in the national social and political standard frame of reference that determine what is ideologically acceptable and, therefore, what ideas are alien and thus enemies of the system.

The strident opposition to the rallies, under the BLM umbrella, was by the white supremacists, by mainstream ideologues, and by the media. This opposition exposed the country's two perennially unsettling questions: the lack of national cohesion as a society, and the forthright inability— actually, refusal—to study and comprehend its history. Whites in the USA have grown up to eagerly and repeatedly dismiss the groaning pain of black people. Black people are to be resisted and controlled and huddled in line. They are to be handled, hunted, and frightened into permanent submission. They are to be controlled, for without stiff physical power these black people will rise -up into resistance and thereby endanger the very existence of white power and white jobs, homes, authority, prestige, domination, pronouncements, acclaim, power, and more power. There has, therefore, been no forthright national effort to imagine a national cohesion centered on true social, political, and economic equality. There has been no national effort to eradicate racism and embrace African Americans in nation-wide social equality.

These several new and old policies remain anchored in a deliberate refusal to accept any history that does not sing and celebrate the glory of the power of the West.

Specifically, knowledge that only elevates the history of the master while negating the value of the oppressed, a nullification that erases the value of African Americans and the roles they played and continue to play in the growth and development of the USA and the West. This nullification thus negates the very existence of racism. Indeed, nullification denies the basis and continued impact of imperialism.

Within the USA, history curriculum in schools across the country is handled at the state, board, district, and county level.

There is no uniform national history at the national level, regarding its veracity and the basis for its multiple claims. This is especially important on the key issues of race, racism, and discrimination and, of course, slavery. And so, a majority of white Americans have gone through school without acquiring any necessary and detailed information about slavery. To be sure, this has also affected the majority of African Americans who have gone through the American school system. Ignorant and ill informed, whites have trooped to and from school completely oblivious as to the origin, extent, and impact of slavery in their own country. (See: Andrew Hacker, *Two Nations: Black and White, Separate, Hostile, Unequal*, New York: Charles Scribner's Sons, 1992.)

Without information, they have grown up refusing to know, denied to know, and eager to defend what they do not know. They have grown up and assumed important positions of authority while remaining ignorant and powerful; eager to make pronouncements on issues and matters of national importance with respect to race and racism that they have deliberately refused or avoided to engage and know. As a result, their pronouncements are an amalgam of distorted information, episodic off- hand tales, imagination, and listening to self -affirming tales on radio and TV, which reinforce the same misinformation that celebrates white supremacy. Without information, without a national effort to know in order to create national cohesion, those in power—the rich, the racists—seek to dismiss the role and impact of slavery and racism in the country. At best, slavery becomes a diluted afterthought. It becomes a largely superfluous institution that had no bearing at all on the USA and the West, and therefore cannot be discussed as part of the rise and permanent impact of racism and poverty and oppression. Hence, ignorance is enhanced and celebrated.

In those moments when the ruling class wishes to appear magnanimous, terrible disturbing statements emerge which reluctantly concede that indeed slavery may have existed, but that this was mild and limited in extent. It was a tragic necessity; that the USA had to have slaves in order to progress, but that even as this was happening, whites were in deep sorrow about slavery itself. And then as soon as it was done, which means as soon as whites had grown rich, the country proceeded to quickly abolish slavery. And America the Innocent grew untouched from such blemish. It once was, but afterwards it never was. Slave owners, which means the country, should deserve credit and praise for pre-planning the end of slavery. You will notice that the short- term and long-term impact of slavery on the country are both side-stepped.

Talking about slavery is seen as an un-American, as an entanglement that does not enhance the narrative of America the Innocent. This becomes essentially a mechanical formula: there were slaves, but then the slave masters graciously released them, having bestowed on them industry, knowledge, hard work, and frugality; slavery was in fact a long -drawn-out apprenticeship. This is, of course, a deliberately insulting imagination now carefully woven in the national mythology and readily embraced by both the white supremacists and the mainstream social, political, and economic structure. No one can understand the rise of virulent racism, the defiant posturing and violence at several levels of the American society, without paying attention to these two permanent realities: that the USA has failed to enhance its national cohesion and that it has deliberately been unable to touch the depth and impact of the institution of slavery. This is where the story must begin.

The energy and seeming defiance from the rallies managed to reach the august corridors of the academy in the USA. On many university campuses, university presidents, provosts, deans, etc. came out to condemn racism and shake their heads at the long perpetuation of this heinous crime upon society and humanity. For this brief temporary moment, African Americans were saluted and hailed; the long -suffering people who have, with dignity, held the ground and pointed this country to the virtues of humanity and the world. And then things get messy and muddy. You can verbally assert your aversion to racism, and then end there. For, after all, to criticize, to oppose, is not to deliver. You can eloquently criticize racism as a theoretical phenomenon while remaining fixed to some form of vague progress. What is required at universities exceeds sheer symbolic gestures. It requires more than symbolic appointments of this or that black person in some relatively senior position at the university. The embrace of Floyd and what his death means must, therefore, be more than symbolism.

The constant theory and strategy of conservative academic institutions has been to step forward and utter stirring words and then go back to the ivory tower and close the doors. From time to time, elaborate pictorials are issued: smiling black students on the football field, or on the basketball court; another one smiling on the lawn with white students; one listening attentively in the classroom, preferably in a laboratory. All of these glossy images are supposed to project and indicate change. What is known, however, is that universities, formulated and funded in racism, cannot engage in wholesale rebellion against racism, let alone the social fabric under capitalism. There will be modifications here and there, but the centerpiece of the institution will remain untouched. At all moments, black students and black faculty will be reminded openly—although now mostly indirectly, but still firmly—that they are essentially foreigners or guests who do not belong. As such, they must be admitted in very small numbers so that they can be seen as a symbol, but forever remaining without importance or power or significance. They can be admitted before their numbers become a problem, then the smiles stop, lips narrow and stiffen, and eyes look away. Thus, the current pronouncements at universities, in response to Floyd, will march on established footprints.

Of equal value to both the academy and corporate institutions is the discovered strategy of Diversity (and Inclusion). In almost all major universities and corporations there are offices and staff geared toward the expansion of diversity; nebulous and amorphous. All of these efforts do not aim to uproot deeply ingrained racism, sexism, oppression, and exploitation. It is also understood that such offices are on the backyard of the institution; that such offices are geared to providing the institution with good publicity and public relations, which can enhance good will and financial profit. At no point is it ever to be imagined that these offices, usually understaffed, will lead to radical change at universities or even corporations. It has now become so clear that what the West values, what its universities and corporations value, is change that produces no change. We have seen this strategy routinely employed on the world stage: a multitude of poor countries who are, in obedience, expected to salute the stated objectives of the West. In the end, the new objectives affirm the old positions of Western power and authority. The West does not have any mechanism or strategy or inclination that envisages the transformation of social, political, or economic institutions that can effectively lead to radical changes ushering in equality and an end of racism. If you agree to change so that you do not change, then that is not change. It is the clever manipulation of structure, institutions, and authority in order to retain power and the historically amassed benefits and advantages.

It is important to bear all this in mind as we shift into a world where the rallies are no longer on the streets. We must avoid the danger of jumping up in the sky whenever this or that institution or corporation comes forward and announces the hiring of a few more black people, or offer financial donations to a few black colleges. Calming the crowds so that rallies are dispersed does not constitute real change. History has shown that this is self-evident. If power remains the same, then there has been no change. What will happen is that there will be enormous force applied to the rallies to compromise, to be reasonable, and to walk slowly on the road to change as stipulated by the system, by the master. This is change that regroups and leads to no change.

The very existence of BLM brings to the fore all the customary problems of definition and change among the oppressed. Capitalism has, through its deep-rooted weapon of cultural imperialism and self-hatred, fear, and force among the oppressed, made it impossible for them to create large-scale resistance. For large-scale resistance to form and expand, there needs to be cooperation, discussions, focus, unity, loyalty, and then the resolve to move away from the master and the system that holds them in poverty and oppression. It entails agreement on the future and a push for it. It accepts the assertion of power and loyalty. It asserts that the oppressed can unite and create another world, their world, and that this world can be led by them independent of the master. This resistance envisages its expansion beyond what *is*, to what *should be*.

Without resistance, the oppressed, the humiliated have tended to ask for basic outcomes: just less oppression, less exploitation, less humiliation, a little bit less brutality. In the absence of moving and agitating for radical change, this becomes a mere search for modification, for little changes, for small alterations, for reforms strongly controlled by the master. This is the appeal, the eternally pleading appeal to the master to bestow some change on the oppressed, and then the oppressed can go back and point to some sort of movement, maybe even possible acceleration on the social ladder. These efforts do not shake the durability, values, power, opinion, and structure of the system. And so, "the struggle continues."

THE RELATIVE VALUE OF CHILDREN UNDER CAPITALISM

I

The character of any society has to be measured by how it treats its children, by how its children are treated and taken care of. The character of individuals surely must be seen in their treatment of children. We, as humans, are born weak and helpless. It takes a long time before we can fend for ourselves (usually dependent on operative social and economic circumstances). We are inherently dependent. We survive through co-dependency. We prosper through co-dependency. Individual triumph, unconnected to other people and circumstances, is therefore a dangerous misleading imperial myth.

The nature of capitalism ensures that from the beginning, different children are valued differently. Children of wealthy parents and lineage are considered more valuable than children of the poor and middling classes. From their entry into the world, class and race determine the fate of children. They are never equal. They cannot be equal. They will never be equal. They are born in different zones and the zones run parallel to each other. Yet capitalist societies have also created well managed and maintained bridges between the zones. These bridges allow for recruitment of cheap labor (in all its variants). That is all. There is no solidarity, no shared visions. Children grow up to be either masters or servants. This is the sad and haunting reality.

What must be quickly understood is that the vision for the future of young people, the vision of the normal, the tolerable, the functional, all of these categories are arrived at in their minds through observation and encounter with the reality around them. This is the power of lived experiences. What is valued, and what is discarded? What is venerated? But above all, what is possible from their position on the bench? The values that shape the young emanate from observable realities. They cannot emulate metaphysical possibilities. They cannot seek for possibilities never encountered, never seen. Survival dictates that they have to quickly master the intricacies of their immediate surroundings. Desperation is reality. Liberal scholars, in moments of condescending elitism, have on occasion referred to this as "street smarts." It is survival. It is a practical reasoned response to the local environment. It is heeding to reality.

What confuses young people, especially poor young people, is the discrepancy between pious declarations of national leaders on the value attached to children and the observable meanspirited, sexist, racist actions and policies that daily mock these pious declarations.

At both a local and a national level, many of these children will quickly note that violence pays, that it can be a neutralizing weapon to wield for survival, on many levels. They also learn that deception, cheating, and violation of rules pays. They are keen observers of the national economic and political culture. They learn that hard work does not necessarily pay; those with the most income and wealth do not necessarily work harder than the rest in their companies or departments. It is clear to them that inherited wealth dominates society and even more revealing is the fact that the wealthy are not necessarily the most intelligent, and certainly not the most generous. They look at their immediate surroundings as schools for survival; they localize and then personalize what they can glean from the national game of domination and survival, a game permanently rigged against the majority.

Capitalist societies get all giddy whenever a few children from the poor classes grow up to attain fantastic success and wealth, in spite of circumstances and environment. This flash of isolated glittering news allows capitalist societies to conveniently forget that these poor children were never allowed to enter the race for life from any point of advantage. Under these circumstances that affect the majority of children in capitalist countries, poverty has to be correctly seen as collective societal violence against children. Capitalist countries live in self-induced fantasy on this question of children and success. They vaguely expect excellent results from no effort; a sort of capitalist miracle of success born out of no attention or effort. Excellent results without investment.

The abuse of children, the selling of children, the exploitation of children, etc. all of these practices, and more, demonstrate the basic weakness of capitalism: lack of care and concern for the welfare of the citizens as people. Children are valued as potential labor, and then as present labor and consumers. Lack of care, lack of concern, lack of societal worry about its children, ensures that all social services geared toward children receive the least amount of investment and resources. Look at the national expenditure in the USA on social welfare and on children, a mere miniscule fraction of the national defense budget, let alone the sprawling military-industrial complex in all of its many divisions and subdivisions. And yet, it is this miniscule amount of budget spent on social welfare and children that is permanently under threat of constant reduction in order to discipline the imaginary ubiquitous "welfare queens" and their children. Look at housing, look at medical attention, and look at the state of medical care for the vast majority of the American children. It is revealing that these inequities (and their real consequences) can be easily and routinely explained away by a society that still perpetually reminds its citizens that they are lucky to be living in "the greatest country in the world."

And then look at the schooling of children. Here, we are of course talking of children of the poor, the workers, the middling classes, that is, the majority of the children. This schooling is an expansive outlay of disjointed half-efforts without coherence. A system of abuse, lack of adequate investment, a system of inherent inequity and ineptitude. Children whose fate is determined by the class and race of their parents. A fate destined to produce different results. A fate which builds and maintains stark and enduring class and racial distinctions. A fate that effectively denies these young people any dream of equal citizenship. They are citizens without the privileges (and even real rights) of true citizenship. Citizens condemned to ride in third-class overcrowded compartments.

Without equal citizenship, there can be no social justice. Without equal citizenship there can be no equal opportunity. Any mention of equal opportunity in the face of unequal citizenship is an insult to the observable reality and to the children who know that they are considered unequal and often made to feel worthless. All the spirited and voluminous pious protestations cannot and will not alter this sad reality.

Starting from shaky and unsteady foundations, these children in essence live in a different country from the children of the rich. They do not breathe the same air. They may not even drink the same water. They have no shared experiences. They have no common frame of reference. They speak and eat differently. They are valued and treated differently.

Class distinctions and divides among the young are maintained, first and foremost, through education. You notice so quickly that any time there is mention of this ever-present and widening gap between the rich and the poor, a chorus of rehearsed condemnation is let loose on TV screens by the rich or their hired emissaries, who suddenly feign indissoluble solidarity with the poor and the excluded. In the USA, the rehearsed refrain is: "We are all Americans. No talk of class warfare." In this way, therefore, the USA becomes a class society with no classes. The miracle of a classless class society. The miracle of the worship of money and class distinctions that produces no serious analysis or discussion of the matter of social class distinctions and their impact on society. The education system, however, dutifully reproduces these class divisions in all of their repetitive configurations.

It can be argued that lack of care for the poor children is deliberate. The reproduction of classes provides a façade of merit winning over mediocre talents or lack of corresponding abilities, the pretense that those at the top deserve to be there due to merit and superior achievements, most evident in superior academic accomplishments. This is the deeply held and well publicized mythology. And so, enrollment in schools and colleges deemed superior and prestigious is tightly controlled. In this way, a mythology of merit is harnessed to justify the ever-present class distinctions. Poor schools lead to poor students, who lead poor lives and then can be easily blamed for their poverty; they did not try hard enough; and they are not gifted or, yes, clever. The system rewards merit.

You have to conclude that capitalism looks at poor children as disposable people. Disposable people available in abundance to provide service to the system in characteristically menial jobs and in the service industry. Disposable people whose fate at the hands of abusers, exploiters, etc. provides material for scholarly books, research articles, public lectures, and newspaper columns; something to hold conferences about, and then provide minimal resources for. This ensures their permanent presence and therefore an endless profitable subject for scholarly output and charity work. Poverty can be quite useful. Here are disposable people whose life circumstances somehow surprise the rich, and on good days even shocks them. Even then, the rich see no organic linkage between their privileged lives bathed in wealth and the pervasive poverty that exists in their society. So close yet so far. Here are a disposable people who, without many attractive alternatives, are led to enroll in the armed forces to protect a society that in reality does not care for them; and has never cared for them. This is the power of power.

II

It is the reproduction of beliefs and tendencies, inclinations, loyalties, etc. that lies at the heart of education in capitalist countries. What remains crucial for these societies is the universalization of imperial values. In doing so, these nakedly oppressive and exploitative values become the national values to be embraced and advanced. The sons and daughters of exploited workers, the struggling middling classes, the excluded, the outcasts, these young people from the other side of the river are recruited to defend a system premised on keeping them and their families, poor and wretched. This miracle is the product of lack of alternatives, education and socialization, actually the acculturation into the ethos of capitalism which masquerades as education. This is a crucial foundation stone for the continued survival of capitalism and imperialism.

A system that in reality devalues those who fight and die in its name. Values that continually affirm the disposable nature of those who fight to defend the system.

And then there are the ever-dwindling job and occupational opportunities. A shrunken or shifting job market forces the unemployed, the underemployed, the youth eager to enter the job market to obediently parade in front of the capitalist employers to work for rates that keep them financially insecure and socially unsettled. The recent and continuing technological advances have, in effect, expanded the category of the labor reserve. This expansion severely limits possibilities of labor organization or unrest. On the contrary, an expanding labor reserve leads to obedience. The poor, the unemployed, the insecure obey in order to be considered for the few jobs available, especially well-paying professional jobs.

Poor children brought up in these circumstances do not have much faith in the future. The children from the oppressed and exploited classes grow up fully aware of the fact that they are not valued, they are not cherished, they are not celebrated. They grow up knowing that their society is really a system of interlocking houses and that they will never have access to the house of power, privilege, and prestige. The powerful routinely invade their over-crowded house looking for sex, workers, and labor. But these poor children can never freely access the house of the powerful, unless by special invitation to render specific service for a defined period. Any effort, any serious effort, aimed at social change must account for this division.

The children of privilege, the valued children, the golden eggs, are brought up to first and foremost defend their social, political, and economic status. They are brought up, they are acculturated and drilled to recite on command, all the high- sounding rationalizations for the existence of their class and status. They are brought up to find meaning and value in oppression and exploitation. They are brought up to see merit in selfishness, and yes, to see merit in imperialism. Specifically in the USA, they are brought up to recite the old narratives about race and why we must celebrate how much progress has been made since slavery in the area of racial discrimination. Indeed, they are brought up to believe that the enjoyment of their wealth and status is enhanced by the presence of the punishing poverty of the majority of the citizens. They are brought up to see the present, this oppressive present, as enlightened progress.

The children of the ruling classes, the owners of the country and the controllers of the society, abhor any talk that meanders in the direction of radical changes, let alone revolutionary changes. They are staunch supporters of tokenism, of slow inconsequential changes that reflect well on them and the system they command. They rejoice in being seen in a positive manner, as interested social patrons who can come and briefly stand with these poor and wretched souls. A brief and well-choreographed encounter with their subjects, their labor, their subordinates. The children of privilege, like their parents, prescribe an unbending work ethic to the poor; a work ethic that they abhor and routinely shun away from.

They preach to the poor to be frugal, hardworking, responsible, accountable, reliable, solid citizens, etc. They prescribe humility, obedience to law and order, truthfulness. No cheating. No stealing.

But these same children of the powerful know that these strictures and prescriptions do not really apply to them. They are members of the house of privilege and power. They belong to a system rigged in their favor. In reality, they operate an armed

gangster establishment rigged in their favor. They deride hard work. Certainly, they cannot see themselves doing hard work. They have hired hands for this sort of thing. This is the work of the children of the poor. Luxury is their constant and consistent value: the pursuit of the good easy life. They see no fellowship between themselves and the children of the poor. They are the children of senior colonial officials ruling over the colonized and the oppressed. From time to time, they invade the wretched world of the poor children looking for sex, drugs, food (exotic food), music, and then afterwards retreat to their colonial enclaves. With the help of modern technology, they can now have most of these delivered to them, thus avoiding the hazardous crossing of the river.

Given these realities and circumstances, the education of the children of the rich has to be seen as an exalted initiation rite that they must undergo before ascending to power, before taking over from their elders. Swallow all the mannerisms of command. Convince yourself to believe all the written and spoken rationalizations for the existence of classes, class oppression, and exploitation. Remember to privately denigrate and then demonize children from the poor classes. In public, however, smile and affirm some vague solidarity with all citizens. They are not your equal, they will never be your equal. They are labor, with bad habits and tendencies. Insist on projecting power that your social station awards you. At no point must the social and economic distance between you and them be erased or interfered with. Be guardian and protector to all schools of thought and thinkers who affirm your position and power and privileges as being natural, logical, and inevitable. Insist in all that you do to affirm that tomorrow will look like today. Reward all of your social and intellectual cheer leaders.

The children of the rich and the powerful will, when the moment arrives, ascend to power and rule, steadfastly upholding the elaborate structures of injustice, oppression, and exploitation. These structures have been decorated with ceremony and rationalization in the form of laws, traditions, and expectations.

Without common aims, it is difficult if not nonsensical to talk of national values and objectives. Whose aims? How did the nation as a composite entity arrive at these aims? If these "established aims" are responsible for promoting and sustaining oppression, discrimination, and exploitation, can they be revised or discarded by the nation? What is clear is that the rich and the powerful have always had the privilege and nasty habit of universalizing their aims, which promote and uphold their political, social, and economic domination. Hired intellectual labor is then deployed to repeatedly frame and popularize the notion that these aims of the rich are also in essence the aims of all the nation. And for this labor these intellectuals are hailed and rewarded. Over time, these intellectuals have reproduced themselves; bringing into being a succession of people espousing the same ideas and then waiting for their turn to be recognized and rewarded for their loyalty to the system.

The behavior of the children of the rich, the children of privilege, is shaped by the socially sanctioned and mandated reward structure. There is reinforcement at home, in the schools, and in the society. In the same way, the social behavior and economic expectations of the children of the poor are shaped by circumstances and socially mandated sanctions: reinforcements at home, in schools, and of course the established discrepancy in the reward structure. Labor of the children of the poor is valued less and rewarded less and rarely, if ever, honored and celebrated. Labor (or strictly, efforts) of the children of the rich, the powerful, is exalted, valued more, celebrated more, and paid more. The reward system keeps the shape of the structure in place.

Education ceases to have any real meaning the moment it becomes a systematic purveyor of a series of rites to be mastered in order to endorse oppression, exploitation, and imperialism as normal and natural. Education ceases to have value the moment the curriculum and social expectations dictate that students and teachers must look at capitalism and imperialism as natural and normal: as a system to be celebrated. We cannot create or work toward creating a good society if our starting point endorses oppression and exploitation as the desirable and compulsory outcome of our efforts.

IN SUPPORT OF HISTORY AND OTHER 'USELESS SUBJECTS'

I

Part of the power of imperialism in Africa, in the Global South, has been visual and cultural, a display marvel of shapes, colors, structures, and material opulence. The intent is to both amaze and, also, incite unquenchable envy and lust for these structures, things and values which are marketed as abundantly omnipresent in the West. In Africa, in the Global South, mired in poverty and oppression, these visuals and glittering images, conveyed through clever electronic marketing and print media, are admiration of abstract constructions; powerful because they are not real, because of their tantalizing abstraction.

We are led into admiring distant visuals and structures that we built and continue to build through imperial exploitation. If you remove the cover, these visuals and structures become offensive reminders of the depth of our oppression and exploitation. The danger lies in projection. We have been forced into believing that all of these structures and material abundance are the product of the ingenuity and hard work of the imperial masters. Look carefully and deeply, and you will see slave trade, slavery, colonialism, neo-colonialism, and now, globalization.

The ruling elite in Africa, in the Global South, permanently uncomfortable with hefty historical questions, have, with characteristic brutal indifference to local circumstances, chosen to close the door to history. Negation seeks to evade acknowledging, touching, seeing, and smelling imperial stains. They look at history as both dangerous and irrelevant. Society can forge ahead without acknowledging its knotted past, let alone its subservient linkage to imperialism. Our condition is really a technical matter; ideology or questions about imperial domination are mischievous intrusions meant to derail the march to progress. Study the correct systems, master digital literacy, expand our profile in the international system and we shall in no time stroll out as free developed countries. Since this is largely a technical problem, we should not waste time agonizing over history and the political economy of our development. Underdevelopment theory and neo-colonialism are obsolete and baseless ill-founded communist inventions. No need for such irritating and useless indulgence. The answers lie hidden in computers.

And so, it has become painfully customary in Africa for politicians, policy experts, educators, and of course the international funding agencies, to dismiss the importance of studying the humanities in schools and colleges. That is, the country should not waste its meager resources on such "useless subjects." This specifically includes history. The way to rapid growth, to development is located in the intricacies and magical revelations of science, mathematics, engineering, technology, computers, and mastery of the World Wide Web.

What has been conveniently forgotten by the ruling elite is the power of imperial humanities in determining the values that have dominated the African imagination, past and present. When the imperialists arrived in Africa, for what has turned out to be a very long visit, they knew that the key to controlling Africans (their values, self-perception, and loyalty to empire) did not lie in science but in humanities writ large. The secret, the enduring secret, for the control of the natives of Africa, of the Global South, continues to reside in the humanities. Initially, it was the Bible. Imperial humanities shaped and conditioned our loyalties, our emotional attachment to imperialists, even our self-definitions. They shaped our world view and frame of reference in interpreting the world. These, in turn, affected our cultures, our relation to our cultures, and our estimation of self, and then our veneration of imperial values, details, symbols, institutions, and accomplishments. In other words, we consume technology within parameters and in advance of values shaped by imperial humanities. Technologies, even at their most triumphant in Africa (and elsewhere), are servants of the "useless subjects." Technologies advance the economic, social, and political objectives, determined, and shaped by the humanities. We must look at this as the first lesson of our reality. We must look at this as the watershed moment of our self-consciousness as a people.

The danger for us, as an oppressed and exploited people, would be to imagine that development and values are not related. The danger for us would be to imagine that our values contained in the humanities, are inherently inimical to economic development. The life-giving critique of the plunder of imperialism lies in the humanities. The critical assessment of cultural imperialism lies in the humanities. It is this cultural imperialism that facilitates continued imperial presence in our midst. The values that we venerate, the objectives that we propose and pursue under imperial guidance are all conditioned and shaped by cultural imperialism.

It follows, therefore, that the supreme objective of our struggle for liberation, must be directed toward self-knowledge, toward conscious and deliberate self-definition. A people tethered to imperial posts cannot claim to be free. We can start on this journey by knowing our history, our cultures and their values, our languages, our foods, our songs, our dances, our art, not as a curiosity, but as an essential element of our being, our deliberate presence. By dismissing some fields of study, courses, and subjects as useless, our neo-colonial leaders are openly declaring war on us, on our cultures, our values, and our future. They are, with determined authority, stating that we should look at our cultures as peripheral to our being as a people. Thus, these values and cultures under siege are or should be seen as inconsequential to our definition, development, and place in the world.

It is the "useless subjects" that are equipped to study, analyze, and critique the pervasive dimensions of cultural imperialism in our societies and show how this phenomenon, now woven into every social and political fabric, forces us into a state of permanent underdevelopment and even self-hatred. The power of the West over us has always been two-pronged: economic domination characterized by plunder and exploitation, and then cultural imperialism. This cultural hold over us in Africa facilitates and thrives on Western economic domination. Cultural imperialism clears the way for economic domination, leading to permanent subordination of us and our societies to imperialism, a steady and redoubtable capture of the mind and spirit. An export of attitudes, inclinations, prejudices, mindset, tendencies. An incredible development that captures the cultural expressions of the oppressed and the dominated. A unique development that sees the oppressed define themselves following the script supplied by the oppressor. A domination that is enduring.

We have also seen that from the colonial period to the present, and especially in the era of globalization, there has been an accelerated migration of Western cultural values, meaning cultural imperialism, from the urban areas to the interior. Peasants in villages who, in the past, may have held onto their ancestral cultures, have started to feel the earth moving underneath their feet. This onslaught is continuous and unrelenting. And so increasingly it has come to pass that to be human, to be modern, one has to display unqualified embrace of Western social and cultural propensities and values. And the old values that held these communities together for centuries are despised, they are mocked and laughed at. All of these attitudes of self-hatred are routinely accompanied by the extension of tentacles of Western economic imperialism in the villages. These tentacles proceed to alter and then destroy peasant economic structures and viability and then the values that both depended on the structures and renewed them.

Cultural imperialism, which decidedly involves intellectual domination, has conditioned us in the Global South to imagine that our political and economic development objectives will succeed to the extent that they are accepted and endorsed by "our friends" in the West. This, as experience and history has repeatedly demonstrated, is false and misleading. This strategy, that "friends" are indispensable for our survival, affirms our subordinate status to the West. Also, this strategy shapes our thinking and reflection on issues concerning our development and existence as independent peoples and societies. As a result, we shun and close our eyes to all those alternatives that may annoy let alone cause ideological discomfort to "our friends." In this way, we hobble ourselves even before we enter the arena of struggle and resistance.

In all of our many struggles for liberation, there are very few examples, if any, of "our friends" in the West participating or choosing to go to war with us as comrades in struggle. There are many examples of distant verbal solidarity, and even this verbal solidarity has been given with many qualifications. In those cases that have involved military confrontation, or extreme civil disobedience and resistance, "our friends" have tended to remain behind or jump off the bus. Resistance to the many facets of cultural imperialism affirms our resolve not to allow the essence and fundamental nucleus of our struggle for liberation to be determined, let alone shaped, by "our friends" in the West. *We* would not presume to define *their* struggles. And, besides, we know that they would never allow us to do so. We know that they would never ever consult us on such matters.

The urge and impulse to seek for the approval of "our friends" in the West arises out of the history of dependency that walks attached to inferiority complex. For to be dependent is to always hide your true identity behind a smiling mask. And this mask becomes your public face. It is assumed that, at some point, in your house or at private functions, you will remove the mask and let your true self, your essence, come out and roar. But it has now become distressingly clear that, for many of the oppressed, this inner self does not come out. The mask, the power of the mask, comes to replace the inner self. The mask becomes the person. And so, tragically, the mask becomes the inner self. In public or private, we only see the mask. The afflicted individual loses the ability to (or even interest in) summon(ing) the inner self to come out and claim the arena--social, cultural, and/or political. The inner self no longer exists, a tragic transformation that is forced onto the oppressed by the power and force of oppression and domination over generations.

But as the inner self recedes and is transformed and fuses with the mask, there arises the crippling affliction of inferiority complex. To subsist and function, inferiority complex comes to rely on several fundamental realities: the oppressed and dominated individual accepts, as a matter of deep undertaking, that he or she is personally inferior to persons who belong to the dominant group, in this case, to whites. That is, at a fundamental level, the oppressed person surrenders and bows. As a group, a collection of individuals who have bowed relinquish resistance, overt and sustained resistance, to this affliction. They come to value survival. This acceptance is transmitted from generation to generation; it is woven in the lessons learned by the youth at the feet of the elders. And not surprisingly, the rationale given by the oppressors and exploiters to justify discrimination and racism strike a fateful- cord among the oppressed. In many cases, the educated among the dominated succumb.

When this reality prevails, as it most often does among the oppressed, there is a very tempting inclination to avoid undertaking any major social/political initiative or program of thought and action without first getting the approval of the master. "Our friends" must vet the initiative, and what they endorse is what is undertaken. But what they endorse reinforces the power of imperialists and their expanded dominance over us and our societies. The struggle for liberation must, therefore, embrace cultural liberation. Liberation for us will remain incomplete without verifiable mental and cultural liberation. This is especially important in all matters pertaining to the youth in Africa.

As much we may condemn the African youth for feverishly seeking to emulate and consume with alacrity Western visual and entertainment culture, we need to remember that the behavior of the youth should be read as a consequence and not the cause of Africa's cultural subordination to imperialism. It is difficult to expect the youth to be indifferent to, let alone, block-out channels of Western culture earmarked for Africa. They are not responsible for constructing these channels, and they see no efforts to challenge their legitimacy and national value. The youth have grown up in societies in which their national leaders have been fervent and faithful caretakers of these channels. And the youth have seen the benefits that accrue from tending them. Can the youth, on their own, resist Western cultural imperialism? How can they do this when the channels are fully functional?

This subordination inevitably translates into economic domination. Cultural habits, preferences, and dispositions find expression in people's consumption habits and yearnings, in what they seek to consume and then the values attached to these items. Cultural habits that venerate the empire will, in turn, despise and deride Africa and Africans. There may be those who will argue, in all seriousness, that all cultures change, and that Africa cannot be the exception. And that what lies in front of us is the emergence of a hybrid, Western-derived culture. Perhaps. But the constant factor in all of this process has been Western domination. In spite of all the veneer of Western acculturation in many areas, Africa is still dominated, with its cultures under siege. Acquisition of Western cultural habits does not, and cannot, diminish the presence and corrosive impact of imperialism.

The study of history, of detailed analysis, the product of original research, brings into focus how we got here. How were our societies shaped and affected by imperialism? History looks for and demands explanations. History peels off the layers of wrapping on the essence of our societies. History forces us to look at our basic realities. The humanities, in the service of the quest for liberation, force us to confront what we are running away from. We cannot, therefore, achieve greatness as African societies if we neglect to come to terms with our objectives for national liberation. Questions about our essence, our values, and our objectives, all are contained in the humanities. We must resist the destruction and erasure of "useless subjects," for without them we shall have no instruments and guides to self-knowledge.

All cultures in the world have produced cultural artifacts, art, and other evidence of their creative output and self-portrayal. Appreciation and value of these cultural productions has, under imperial domination, varied immensely. The variation is principally connected to the operative commercial value of these productions. Art and creative productions have, even more than before, become money on canvas.

Under the imperial system of value, Western art and artistic productions have, as expected, been deemed more valuable than all others, especially African cultural productions. And so Western artists, "the masters," have their works valued above African art. This art is purchased not necessarily to be publicly displayed for public enjoyment, but as investment. From time to time, it will be let out of its secure hide-out for temporary exposure in museums on a limited basis. And, like everything else under capitalism, the West has the decisive voice on the matter of value of items, of commodities for purchase and trade. This investment follows a well- established pattern: West rules.

This imperial framework for determining the value of art ensures, as a matter of necessity, that art from Africa by Africans is valued less. While we know that Western artists whose work is over-celebrated and valued—for example, Picasso—based their art on African masters, African art nonetheless commands minimal value in imperial-dominated markets. This art becomes "primitive art" or "tribal art" or "vernacular art," etc. The pattern of the past still dominates commerce and determination of value of cultural productions.

And yet, Western museums are full of art and artifacts from the Global South. All major Western museums contain African art, including pieces from ancient Egypt of the Pharaohs. This is art that was not paid for; work of inestimable value that was acquired for free at the point of a gun. To see it, to see our past cultural productions, we must travel to the West. How many of us can travel to the West for this purpose? These African cultural treasures have not and will not disturb the endurance of Western racism.

In the struggle for African liberation, we must state as a matter of urgency that *we* shall determine the value of our art. We must move away from the economics of dependency, which allows the West to both acquire our art while simultaneously undervaluing it. In the Western world, forever influenced with bigotry and racism, our art will always be confined to several places below their art, even if their art is derived from our masters. This is racism. This is imperialism. Thus, it is crucial for us, as part of our liberation, to encourage, value, and cherish our artists (of all mediums) and proceed to display their art for our enjoyment and celebration. Our art, like Western art, will be in response to our immediate circumstances and realities. This, of course, also applies to creative literary arts.

As part of our deliberate efforts to demonstrate our pride in our arts, we must proceed to erect and maintain, at a high level, museums, and theatres. This must be seen as a top priority in our liberation. Museums, cultural houses, and related structures, maintained at a high impeccable level, must showcase our cultural productions of the past and the present. It is a matter of everlasting shame that the current neo-colonial regimes in Africa have failed to see this as a crucial non-negotiable national objective. Our cultures and their values cannot survive on their own. They were not formed on their own, independent of society. Indeed, Western cultures do not survive on their own. They are grafted onto commerce, economics, propaganda, fantasy, education, politics, and linkages to the capitalist system and its values.

The matter of retrieving our cultural treasures currently held in imperial museums and homes must be tackled as part of the compound objective of our cultural renewal and rededication, which will lead to extensive investment in our museums, archives, and cultural houses and outlets, all maintained at high impeccable levels. We bring them home to celebrate them. We bring them home to honor them and remember the ingenuity of the artists and the societies that produced them. This is the new cultural awakening that works in concert with our drive toward liberation.

At all times and at every level, we must insist on linking culture, cultural productions, values, etc. to our quest for liberation. To this end, therefore, we cannot and must not seek to endorse or support those values whose essence and meaning work against our chosen path of national and Pan-African liberation and our march toward socialism. There are men in power in neo-colonial countries who eagerly endeavor to codify those regressive aspects of cultures that reinforce patriarchy and male chauvinism. A conscious effort must be made to denounce and then resist any expressions of gender tyranny or sexism as aspects of treasured traditional values. We affirm that African cultures have more cherished values, more enduring progressive values. We seek to treasure and cherish our past without being tricked into reinforcing oppression, which, in the end, facilitates and sustains imperial domination.

II

The ruling elite in the Global South, and especially in Africa, have, as part of their rationale for facilitating shameless imperial plunder, argued that they do not want their countries to be left behind, that they seek to modernize their countries along Western lines. The theory behind these speculative efforts holds that these poor oppressed and exploited countries will emerge, after some indeterminate period, resembling Western capitalist countries in power and wealth. A tantalizing and even seductive mirage. It has never happened. It cannot happen. This is, therefore, poisonous fruit.

Leaders seeking to evade social responsibility for dwindling prospects for employment, especially of the youth, have loudly proclaimed that all these problems can be attributed to the pervasiveness of "useless subjects" in schools and colleges, and that, for these reasons, the teaching of these subjects must either be severely curtailed or abolished.

These same rulers travel overseas and are mesmerized by the beauty of imperial memorials, museums, theaters, colleges, public parks, etc., all meticulously cared for by various levels of government agencies (direct and indirect). Deliberate or not, these rulers fail to see the direct and purposeful linkages between imperial aims and these objects, institutions, and memorials. Imperial states place a lot of emphasis on memorials and historic structures as visual displays of imperial objectives, might, and achievements. The value of these memorials as an integral part of self-definition of these imperial societies cannot be denied.

Thus, "useless subjects" are of great value at the center of empire. They shape the world view of the next generation of imperial masters. Each succeeding generation of imperial masters receives instruction on the values to uphold through the "useless subjects." Why the system must be upheld and the rationale for empire, all of these are relayed via the "useless subjects." These subjects shape the loyalty of each new generation to the capitalist imperial system. African countries seek to erase the "useless subjects," even as the imperial center desperately upholds the power of its own history, memorials, and definition.

Even those who come to "invent technologies," they too are shaped by the values conveyed through the "useless subjects" in their countries. This is especially true in regard to their loyalty to capitalism and imperialism and the values that propel these systems locally and internationally. New technologies are absorbed and incorporated into an already established framework: to advance and protect Western economic and cultural dominance.

What technologies do is to facilitate the advance of imperialism. What technologies do is to tether even more firmly the Global South to the centers of the empire. What technologies do is to deepen the extent of imperial involvement in almost all affairs in the Global South. The reach of technologies, advertised as indispensable, forces the Global South into belonging to a club it cannot resign from, a club in whose governance it has no voice, a club that seeks no input from the Global South.

The operative danger ever on the lips of the ruling elite in Africa has been to imagine that technology alone leads to development. That importation of Western technologies, haphazard and uncoordinated, will propel these societies into shining technical wonderlands. It is vital to mention here that inventors of varieties of technologies, from cell phones to computers, etc., have been very adept at marketing their products as "must have" items. These technologies, and the accompanying skills, have been touted as indispensable problem solvers, as keys to the kingdom.

Yet we know that even in the Western countries, home of these technologies, the original social, economic, and political problems still abound. Poverty, violence, racism, sexism, unemployment, class distinctions, and corresponding class oppression and exploitation, all of these and their multiple social repercussions, still cover the expansive texture and structures in the West.

The poor and the oppressed in Western societies are avid consumers of these new technologies and inventions. Cell phones, etc., are on open display. To be sure, there is what has come to be termed as the "digital gap" between the rich and the poor in these countries in the possession and use of these technologies. But these technologies are not absent in poor homes and neighborhoods. The gap lies in extent and volume and purpose. In other words, the pattern of the possession and consumption (utilization) of these technologies has not deviated from pre-existing structures of race, power, wealth, and class. Technologies have reinforced these pre-existing structures and patterns. Technologies have reinforced the power of capitalism and imperialism. Technologies have reinforced preexisting racial differentials in power and wealth and have thus played a very conservative and even regressive role.

And we must always remember that these new technologies have a notorious and troublesome history of exploiting labor in the Global South. Many of the mass-produced and mass marketed gadgets are assembled in the Global South for shameful wages, with workers toiling under intolerable conditions. New technologies, like the old technologies, are great beneficiaries of oppression and exploitation of the Global South. And, as usual, they will never tolerate nor nurture consequential competition from the Global South. New technologies are marketed to the Global South for profits and not to create new Silicon Valleys. This is an imperial constant.

Countries in the Global South are immensely attracted to these new technologies and proceed to invest immense national resources to this shining magic. You notice quite quickly that this impulsive reaction leads to uncoordinated and haphazard introduction of these technologies in varieties of fields, firms, and establishments. As in the past, these importations and deployments are uncoordinated, with no easily discernible national focus. There is an almost juvenile urge to be seen playing with the latest toy, the latest shining toy. There is some social pride derived from being able to show competency in handling the latest toy. Resources spent training the youth on the intricacies of these technologies are really a form of financial donation to the Western countries. For, in many cases, the youth cannot attain local employment and so they migrate or remain local to be employed cheaply in local assembly plants or call centers of Western corporations.

There is no evidence to support the theory that superabundance of computer technicians, programmers, and even engineers will lead to a new, vibrant, self-sustaining economy in these countries. And since the shelf life of these qualifications is not so elastic, it becomes necessary to continually retrain and update information and skills. In the imperial countries, there are many such people, quite often unemployed or under-employed at much junior positions. New technologies have not solved the inherent contradictions of capitalism in regard, to, labor, poverty, consumption, discrimination, oppression, class, and exploitation. An emphasis on the "useful subjects" in essence seeks to strategically evade asking the hard and uncomfortable questions about these key facets of society: mismanagement of the national economy, class, disparities in wealth and income distribution, imperial exploitation, social justice, gender equality, corruption, national stagnation, political repression, and lack of national definition.

In Africa, history rescues the nation from distortion, from polished yet erroneous mythologies. History brings to the surface those uncomfortable details that have been evaded or avoided in order to create current dazzling shiny mythologies that have in the end left the country on its knees. Mythologies that have conspired against nationhood, economic liberation, national purpose, people's power, social justice, and local cultures. The revolutionary historian in Africa recovers lost knowledge, packages this knowledge, and presents it to the nation in order that it may find its purpose and stand up.

THE PITFALLS OF HALF-REVOLUTION

I

Can we have, as our objective, the quest for a Half Revolution, halfway between liberation and imperial plunder? If you were to listen to many of our educated elite, you would quickly find that when they want to appear progressive, they will reluctantly embrace this strategy. They regard this as a reasonable concession on their part. Now who can dare accuse them of being anti-progressive change in Africa? Here they are embracing sets of alternatives aimed at enhancing the welfare of the masses.

This strategy of Half-Revolution is close to the so-called Third Way in Western political theoretical formulation (and speculation), standing between socialism and capitalism. The imagined outcome here is that the Third Way will be most acceptable and treasured, for, after all, it will have trimmed off both the particularly noxious excesses of capitalism and also cut off Marx's beard. The outcome, it is hoped, will be a miracle: an agreeable ideology that will leave the present structure of capitalism largely undisturbed, except for minor adjustments and rearrangements. (See: Anthony Giddens, *The Third Way: The Renewal of Social Democracy*, Cambridge, UK/Malden, MA: Polity Press, 1999.)

Here, therefore, you have the pronouncements of feeble and non-consequential change. In essence, change that leads to no change. For, indeed, what the proponents of the Third Way want is not a revolution against capitalism and imperialism. They do not want any serious and drastic changes in society. They shudder at the very thought of causing massive social changes in the society's class structure. This is not what they want or are scheming for. (See: Alex Callinicos, *Against the Third Way*, Cambridge, UK/Malden, MA: Polity Press, 2001.)

It should be mentioned that the proponents of the Third Way are the educated elite and sections of the ruling elite, who seek to sound clever over miniature configurations, even if these minute contributions are announced with fanfare and their authors are rewarded with honors, money, titles, etc. And herein lies the problem. The danger for progressive forces is to imagine that their contributions are invalid until they are recognized by the governing class and structure.

The Third Way is the brainchild of imperial benevolence, a willingness to be seen to be caring and concerned for the welfare of the poor and the disadvantaged, the fiction that, after all, imperialism listens and is willing to change its ways. It is flexible enough to respond to social needs of the poor and other marginalized groups. Let us, however, call it for what it is: a deliberate conspiracy against revolutionary change and revolutionary impulses in society. The Third Way seeks to reinforce imperialism and not overthrow it. The solutions are seen as deeply embedded in capitalism and imperialism. As a result, the Third Way counsels against revolutionary changes and efforts. It aims to refurbish the image of capitalism and make it wholly acceptable even by its historic victims, thus delegitimizing any advocacy of radical changes and revolution. In other words, the Third Way seeks to reinforce the power and durability of imperialism.

This strategy of the Third Way is, of course, anti-history, anti-knowledge. Its foundation lies steeped in fantasy, deceit, and fast-talking delusion. None of the proponents of the Third Way can point to any instance or historical situation whereby imperialism reformed itself so much and so willingly, as to become the "people's imperialism." And what does that mean? None of the defenders of the Third Way can point to historical instances in which imperialism became the engine of consequential social justice aimed at erasing the power and privileges associated with a stubborn class structure. What we see are efforts to confuse, confound, and conflate. The heart of the matter is that imperialism cannot on its own be any other thing, other than imperialism. No amount of superficial trimming, excited expansion of this or that social amenity, means anything if the economic structure is left intact. It is this structure and the social fabric woven around it that produce the problems in society, including poverty, which the Third Way seeks to superficially address.

The starting point in the drive for Half-Revolution is to imagine (for it remains at the level of imagination) that the inherited colonial capitalist system under imperialism can be tamed and reformed so as to become responsive to solving problems linked to poverty, powerlessness, and exploitation in African countries; that, therefore, the inherited system can, through a series of clever manipulations, be employed to erase poverty, landlessness, poor schools, poor health care, etc.; and that this laudable outcome can be achieved without in any way fracturing this inherited system. We can simultaneously have a well-defined oppressive and exploitative class structure, while also undermining its integrity by clever redistribution. In other words, imperialism can both plunder and redistribute; it can oppress and liberate. It can both exploit and embrace aggressive redistribution. That equality (of sorts) and social justice can emerge from Half-Revolution.

The embrace of the notion of Half-Revolution is, of course, a conspiracy of the elite against African peoples and societies. It is not very different from the half-baked ideas pushed under the modernization theory, that were rapidly adopted by many of the first leaders of independent African countries. Half-Revolution posits that in fact progress, dignity, and liberation can all be achieved in Africa within the bosom of imperialism. Therefore, imperialism should not be seen as the enemy; rather, with adequate technical expertise, social justice, equality, solidarity, and progress for the people can after all be achieved in Africa without expelling imperialism. The elite will, at this point, be quick to point to South Korea, Taiwan, Singapore, etc. as shining examples of this magical formula. It is significant that this effort is not immediately accompanied by a thorough historical analysis. Specific details and analysis pertaining to these examples are rarely attempted, for indeed they would show why they have not been duplicated across the Global South.

But then again, this reluctance to engage history and historical circumstances and context, should not appear as a shock. A painful characteristic of imperialism and its advocates is a deliberate avoidance of engaging critical analytical history. Rather, what is favored are weighty and enormous pronouncements standing independent of history. These are then immediately universalized so as to apply to all societies. The West has been successful, through multiple forms of domination, in ensuring that its academic texts are adopted by the Global South, as locally and internationally relevant and applicable. Such knowledge is universal. But knowledge from the periphery, from the Global South, is denied entry into the cannon. It is too local, too specific, too incidental, too unproven, too African.

This point is repeatedly illustrated by the dismissal of the value of local African expertise by Western scholars and governments. African experts are not trusted nor are they routinely called upon to give expert opinions in areas of their expertise in their own countries. In fact, being local is held against them; they cannot be relied upon to be objective. This position is held onto, in spite of their polished credentials attained at leading Western universities and institutions. It is almost as if Western knowledge gets tarnished and loses its value the moment it is conferred on the African, the local. It becomes suspect, its market value plummets. At best, they can be local consultants, which means they have minimal power regarding the outcome of the assignment or project.

Key conclusions and binding directives will be drafted far away from the local scene. Knowledge and credentials are not enough to steer the imperial system to work in favor of African development and progress. Built into this system is a lever that forever shuts us out from discussions and decisions in the "big house," from the floor of power. We are, at best, confined to the children's table.

The fear of the ruling elite in African countries is simple: they fear losing all the loot, all the heavy and boundless loot, the product of their long-lasting brazen theft and plunder. For those who care at all, there is an ensuing struggle, fueled by fear, to tame the anger of the hungry masses while retaining the bulk of their wealth. This is the Christmas strategy. Appear generous and caring at Christmas time (or similar festive occasion) and ensure that you are photographed distributing gifts and foods to the poor wretched souls, and then disappear never to be seen again until next Christmas. But is this enough? How about perennial problems of housing, food, gender inequality, landlessness, employment, school fees, health care, security, etc.? There is something very disturbing here. The poor and the disenfranchised are expected to readily salute in gratitude, but never to question why they are poor, and why they have become objects of sporadic minimal charity.

Conceptually, the strategy of Half-Revolution looks at imperialism having a permanent presence in Africa; that it can never be over-thrown, and the ruling elite will steadfastly ensure that the status quo remains undisturbed. The ruling elite (and the educated elite) argue with passion how imperialism can be made to work for the people. After all, isn't this true in the USA or UK or other Western powers? They live in a world of fantasy fueled by selfish economic and political considerations, which they have labeled as national interests. In this, we see why Half-Revolution is a decided enemy of the African masses and an elaborate obstacle to what Africa can be.

There are many African educated elites (which include scholars and journalists), and especially politicians, who have become local voices and activists in support of the Western ideological struggle against radical nationalism and communism. They repeat, almost verbatim, many of the standard phrases and tools of promotion and advertisement of capitalism manufactured in the West and disseminated in Africa, as the basis of their objections against socialism, let alone communism. In this matter, to follow directives, direct or indirect, from the center of the empire is to affirm our own irrelevance. In supporting imperialism and its interpretation of history, and especially of our conditions and realities, we affirm the long-standing Western position that holds us as intellectual juveniles in search of grooming, direction, guidance, and approval. On this central issue, we should actively remember that no matter how elegant our discourses might be, the stubborn and painful reality is that all tracts and utterances in support of capitalism also support imperialism. Such tracts and efforts provide evidence of our learned ignorance and shocking self-hatred, all in the service of our historical oppressors and exploiters.

In practical terms, the strategy of Half-Revolution endorses the exploitation of Africa's raw materials by imperialism. It sanctions and protects the exploitation of

Africa's resources by agents of imperialism. This strategy supports the continued underdevelopment of Africa and Africans. It also looks for expertise on these matters from the centers of Western imperialism. Operationally, this strategy fully supports the current distribution of power, i.e., with the West at the helm of this imperial system. Half-Revolution concedes, as a matter of necessity, that Africa is powerless and will always be powerless. This is seen as being realistic. It is, therefore, a strategy of weakness that somehow looks at Africa's lowly status and weakness as an enlightened position to uphold. Half-Revolution must be seen as a deliberate betrayal of all past hopes, current hopes, and future hopes for African liberation.

A crucial matter sidestepped by Half-Revolution concerns the personal dimensions of oppression and exploitation of Africans by imperialism. We are the despised and the humiliated. We have, for centuries now, been dismissed by Western imperialism as inferior and historically inconsequential. We have carried this burden, this pain, over hundreds of years. The pain that is deep and enduring. We are the people who live in constant fear of being humiliated in front of our children or loved ones: on the continent or in the diaspora. The constant realization that for us living is indeed a struggle, a dogged struggle to survive; a life of perpetual combat to survive. That we live in fear, we even plan in fear. And this affects our health, our relationships, our progress, our sense of self, our reflections, our image of the future. All this we cannot share. And indeed, when we talk or seek to be heard, we are ignored, dismissed, and again humiliated. It is this sense of powerlessness, this patrolled silence under imperialism, that dominates our reflections about this world and our place in it.

Institutions of Western imperialism are constructed to ignore any such concerns and worries from the oppressed and the exploited, in the Global South. It is taken for granted that opinions from the oppressed, cannot be given prominence at the imperial table. On all issues and reflections that affect the fate of the world, the fate of billions of people in the Global South, it is taken as routine and normal that all opinion makers, all the authoritative voices, are located in the West. Distinguished 'talking heads,' newspaper columnists, TV panels, leading academic figures and public intellectuals, think tanks, etc.—all these are overwhelmingly Western. The rest of the world, especially the Global South, is not even allowed a brief look into the inner chamber. We are expected to cheer but never to offer any opinion, and there are consequences for venturing to oppose the master, even if this concerns our lives, and especially if this touches on our livelihoods. The ideas that matter are all Western. Beyond the economic aspects of imperialism, this stranglehold on instruments of international affairs and commerce, has to be seen as the indisputable demonstration of Western hegemony. And so, the offender, the bully, the criminal gets to determine what can and cannot be written and debated about his crimes, and even the definitions allowed. Under these circumstances, Western institutions of international affairs and commerce seek not investigate, analyze, and change, but rather to continually repair the dam so that it does not break. Rewards are swiftly given to all those able to suggest the best ways of repairing the dam. Here is where foreign aid comes into the picture.

Foreign aid is and has always been a powerful imperial weapon, routinely employed to ensure enduring absolute obedience by the oppressed and the exploited. Poverty, the result of imperial plunder and avarice, is used as a weapon to ensure the obedience of Africans. The strategy of Half-Revolution evades addressing how much, in real terms, Africa has paid for this insignificant foreign aid. For indeed, it is most relevant to inquire about the political, economic, and social cost of foreign aid to Africa. Should foreign aid, in all of its totality, be seen as adequate compensation for all past and current imperial plunder?

We, in the Global South, we in Africa, have been conditioned to believe as an article of indisputable faith, that we cannot operate or survive without foreign aid. That foreign aid is, well, indispensable. What is missing from this theology are contributions from the locals, the oppressed peasants, and workers. Their voices are shut out from surveys, analyses, and formulations. All those elegant figures and tables presented in glossy publications, rarely, if ever, include the voices of the people bound to endure the negative effects of foreign aid.

Why does the camera and the flashlight veer away from the victims of foreign aid? The clearest evidence of the non-democratic nature of foreign aid is that the majority of the citizens are not consulted on choices, priorities, volume, impact, and implications of that aid. Foreign aid is an externally imposed solution. Having been declared as indispensable, the natives, the laboring multitudes, are then assembled to sing in loud voices songs praising the givers of foreign aid to the country. These songs must keep coming even when there is clear evidence of injuries and incurable harm wrought on their society by foreign aid. The prisoners and the oppressed must dance for the master, for then we can all pretend that there is no prison, there is no oppression. Half-Revolution is conceptually and operationally unable to stop citizens of these African countries from being forced to sing songs of praise for imperialism as they march to their graves in poverty.

All those wedded to the realism of Half-Revolution must, as a test of the popularity of their positions, subject foreign aid to a rigorous local exposure, inquiry, debate, and consideration. Who will provide the critical justifications, and who will be left with the duty of enumerating the benefits of foreign aid to the hungry masses? We miss the point of democracy when we actively seek to impose policies on the poor masses for the good of the ruling elite, especially when it is evident that these policies deepen their poverty and oppression. There is no policy that is so complex as to be beyond the comprehension of the masses. No objective aimed at the masses can be too complex for them to consider its essence, impact, and implications. To argue thus is to take a colonial outlook toward the African people.

What would happen if African countries refused to accept foreign aid as currently constructed and implemented? What would happen if these countries decided, collectively, to renounce the now well-established practice of accepting conditional foreign aid that undermines national sovereignty, deforms the national agenda for development, and facilitates the entrenchment of imperialism in Africa? Can we talk about this?

Foreign aid entrenches not only the inherited system of colonial capitalism, but it also reinforces the notion that there is no other way. It forecloses, and therefore foregoes, any and all national imagination for alternative ways to reconstruct national economies aimed at expelling imperialism. Why have African intellectuals, especially African economists, allowed themselves to be trapped in this mirage? Can we talk about this?

In the march toward the African revolution, away from the futility of Half-Revolution, we shall reiterate our position of dismissing the supposed positive impact of foreign aid and other activities of Western financial institutions on the lives of our people. The presence of a few Africans within the ranks of the World Bank, the International Monetary Fund, the World Trade Organization, and other such organizations, will not and cannot in -itself change the fundamental objectives of these institutions as custodians and guarantors of Western imperialism and its domination over Africa and the Global South. There may be a few modifications, but they are superficial in the sense that they do not shake the unchanging objectives of international imperialism presided over by these organizations. Our condition and our fate are not altered by the presence of a few high-ranking African employees within these agencies. Individual achievement and glory, however tempting when hailed and publicized in imperial circles, cannot lead to national liberation and development. We must, therefore, refrain from the unfortunate habit of extending our hands into submission and compromise (all smiles), whenever our cousins, sisters, and country homeboys are appointed to some positions in these imperial organizations. The imperial system, our eternal oppressor and exploiter, remains in place and continues to fervently reproduce itself.

II

There are two important questions concerning the future of Africa that are not directly addressed by Half-Revolution: the furious destruction of our environment, and racism. At the moment, we cannot have any serious movement toward our liberation and development without coming to terms with the collective impact of these issues on our lives.

We should immediately note that the current environmental crisis is associated with the growth and expansion of capitalism and imperialism. Western development has been intimately linked to and associated with environmental destruction, not only in the West, but also in those areas in the Global South that were either directly under Western colonial rule or Western economic domination. Capitalism is inherently predatory; it carries with it a predisposition to destroy in order to accumulate; a tendency to disregard environmental protection in favor of immediate profits and advantages. The result has been a wanton criminal destruction of the environment. Of course, the linkage between history and environment is not a new subject. Ancient societies paid a heavy price for careless destruction of their environment. What makes this current destruction stand out is its sheer scale, intensity, and escalating consistency. This has become an international problem. All humans and non-humans are now affected. For many poor workers and peasants in Africa and in the rest of the Global South, they are now forced to suffer the outcomes and by-products of this environmental calamity that they neither caused nor benefited from. This is the ugly side of imperialism, rarely discussed at forums and other elegant gatherings.

The West has, via agencies under its control, emerged as the primary advocate of environmental protection. To be sure, there are many strong political and corporate voices that remain opposed to any form of consequential protection of the environment. Current efforts aimed at environmental- protection, nonetheless, raise several disturbing questions, especially as they touch the future of our continent. The general implications of these efforts are to leave in place established economic advantages enjoyed by the West under this system of imperialism. Save the environment but do not dare touch on current Western economic domination. This has led to some grumbling and forms of push -back from countries in the Global South engaged in rapid efforts toward aspects of industrialization. These countries want to attain what the West has: vibrant industrialized societies. Now let us be clear here. These protestations are not on behalf of the people in the Global South, but rather on behalf of the ruling elite, rich barons, and more crucially, on behalf of foreign multinational corporations. The West is still featured in these protestations. For after all, these countries seek to attract foreign investment, which overwhelmingly refers to Western corporations. And as part of the conditions for installing subsidiaries in these countries, multinational corporations demand and get most lax regulations on matters related to environmental protection. They pollute and destroy the environment with impunity, including the dumping of hazardous waste in some countries in the Global South.

The West seeks to uphold and protect capitalism and imperialism; this system that it dominates. This is the system that awards the West the majority share of the world's economic benefits. The world must, therefore, be saved for capitalism and the West. Under this rubric, a green world, the green economy, as currently imagined and occasionally defined, would still be adamantly capitalist and therefore in support of imperialism. We, in Africa, would still be victims of this new version of imperialism. Tomorrow's world, hopefully environmentally conscious, would still be imperialist. We shall still be hanged, even if this time the ropes and the nooses will be made from wholly recycled and eco-friendly materials.

What has been deliberately side-stepped and ignored are the inherent contradictions in the positions taken by the West on this question. We start by acknowledging the obvious: that the bulk of the environmental calamity can be placed at the feet of capitalism and imperialism, and the ensuing capitalist values and emphasis (in both production and consumption), in labor relations, etc. In order to correctly address the question of environmental destruction, we need to revisit linkages between: capitalism and production, between capitalism and consumption, between capitalism and labor, between capitalism and exploitation, between capitalism and oppression, between capitalism and land, and between capitalism and justifications for environmental destruction. To proceed toward environmental protection without addressing these toxic linkages is to engage in deliberate deception. Can we protect the environment while simultaneously affirming and expanding the system most responsible for this calamity? Why are we expecting different results? Can, in this instance, the destroyer become the protector? How can an unrepentant destroyer, set on escalating destruction, become the protector of the environment? Imperialism has, with deliberate indifference to all evidence confirming destruction of the environment, condemned humanity to this cruel fate: capitalism or nothing, which means capitalism and death. And so, the Amazon and other forests burn, and we are forced to wring our hands and shift uncomfortably in our chairs in silence, all in salute to the rugged rigor of the free enterprise system.

The presence of neo-colonial regimes in Africa, adherents to capitalism and imperialism, raises urgent questions about environmental protection on the continent. Environmental destruction constitutes a present danger to the security of Africans. Destruction of grass cover, forests, and grasslands; poisoning of rivers and water basins; decimation of wild -life, etc.—all these and more create unmatched insecurity of our people and their livelihood. These consequences call into question the very survival of communities and their centuries-old cultural values and traditions.

Demands for raw materials from Africa have made it difficult to limit areas and forms of cultivation, and this in turn bleaches the soils and then expands the cruel reality of desertification. The pursuit of capitalist development, dripping in selfishness and with no regard for its consequences, leads to greedy destruction of plants and forests, and gives rise to soil erosion. At the end of all this is the mirage, the fictitious claim, that indeed all humanity can be capitalist, that all humanity can enjoy a share in the current standards of living in the West and eat and consume and burn with no limitations. Capitalism for all under imperialism.

It is easy to expose the fallacy of this claim by looking at the Western societies themselves. Class, gender, and race have all converged to deny a large portion of Western citizens from enjoying the reputed "Western life-style." In other words, they live in the West, they are citizens of many of these countries, but they do not lead the "Western life-style." The majority do not live in endless luxury in, for example, four- or more bedroom homes, own multiple expensive cars, vacation in the Alps, have access to a clean environment, own vacation homes, have hundreds of thousands of dollars in cash in banks or retirement accounts, regularly dine out in expensive restaurants or eat several gourmet meals at home prepared in state-of-the-art, expansive kitchens. No, they do not. We do have a situation here whereby there is a deliberate distortion of reality through propaganda, in order to sell and justify a fantastic mythology and mirage. It would thus be wrong to base our national policies of development on this mirage. We cannot and must not be lured by mythology into committing ourselves and our countries to eternal poverty and misery while we subsist under imperial domination.

It is, however, going to be very difficult to vigorously protect the environment in Africa and the rest of the Global South, as long as these countries seek to retain their status as appendages of imperialism. Multinational corporations, protected by Western governments and international financial and commercial agencies, will continue to make environmentally destructive demands. Further, the greedy and treasonous ruling elite in these countries will continue to facilitate the ruinous operations of multinational corporations. And we should not forget that in some cases these countries have virtually lost ownership and control of their natural resources, including land. Under such circumstances, the multinational corporations own the country and have a decisive voice in its economic and political destiny. Lack of ownership of national assets, including education, drastically reduces the power to initiate and expand local environmental policies (assuming that some do exist or have been considered). The quest for national liberation, for African revolution, must be linked to credible and durable environmental protection.

From its inception, capitalism has never been held back by small inconvenient details like protection of the environment or adequate compensation of labor. It has never lost sleep over these concerns. This disposition to be careless, to be wantonly destructive, has been helped by several factors. Chief among these factors is the matter of the geography of environmental crimes. Ordinarily, the capitalists, the captains of industry, do not live close to where their businesses are located or where the environmental destruction takes place. They do not live next to the forests being destroyed or next to the rivers being polluted, or the refineries poisoning the air. They reside far away, a comfortable distance from the scene of their crimes. They and their social and economic class maintain a safe distance from these environmental crimes. And so, we see oil refineries—and industries linked to these refineries—located next to highways or in locations close to poor neighborhoods, occasionally within those actual poor neighborhoods. These enterprises, central to capitalist economy, have a devastating impact on the poor; whose water is poisoned, air polluted, and soils rendered unfit for habitation or agriculture. In these neighborhoods, children are born with multiple health problems and thus denied any chance of leading happy productive lives. The total impact on the poor is grave: poverty is recycled along with poor health.

On those rare occasions when the cries of the poor push through to become public knowledge, thus meriting temporary attention, an obligatory commission of inquiry is set up, often returning a verdict of "not guilty" or "inconclusive." Either the industries are not to blame, or the harm is negligible. But if the harm is so negligible, and if these industries are "not guilty," and if all that these industries do is so good for society, then why are they all located in poor neighborhoods? Why are they not located next to their owners, in the rich and posh neighborhoods?

The poor have paid for capitalist development on many levels: in being exploited, underpaid, overworked, and working under hazardous conditions performing dangerous jobs. They have paid with their health, as a myriad of diseases and health conditions continue to have a devastating impact on their physical and mental health. Here, we see the results of both physical and mental oppression. In almost every case, and at every turn, these multiple effects on the poor are never discussed as part of the endless price of capitalist development, part of the injurious impact of capitalism on the society. Can we start here?

In the Global South, the ruling elite, the prefects of the local imperial enterprises, also reside far away from the scenes of environmental destruction and pollution. And they do not even have to visit these areas. They do not have to see the slaughter of wildlife and pollution of rivers and destruction of forests and soils. All they want, all they have ever wanted, are ample funds deposited in their overseas accounts. The ruling elite can, therefore, afford to look the other way, to pretend, to live in comfortable suspension. As for the multinational corporations, they can afford to pretend that in fact they are doing a lot of good in Africa: they provide employment and bring light to these accursed countries. And they come back to this point again and again as their fundamental rebuttal against any, and all criticisms. All of this takes place in London, New York, Tokyo, Beijing, Berlin, Paris, Rome, Lisbon, Madrid, Brussels, etc. It is easy to pretend that all is well, for after all you do not see the rumored suffering. This behavior, endemic to capitalist enterprises, amounts to destruction without consequences. Destruction without care. After all, this takes place far away from you.

The nature of capitalist economies is to afford all corporations and the business community as many financial advantages and as many legal protections as possible. The business community stands above all else in society. It is repeatedly emphasized that it is this community that is the engine of progress in the country and the world. On their own, corporations disdain regulations and any sanctions imposed to protect communities, especially poor communities. But people's welfare, including their health, must, in a humane society, take priority over profits and profit margins. Pollution, poisoning of air and water, deforestation, poverty, violence, and hopelessness cannot be indicators of development, even if all of these are strongly asserted by the corporations, academic experts, international financial agencies, and governments. It has now been continually demonstrated that capitalism does not have the ability to solve its contradictions; it cannot clean up after itself.

On some very basic and fundamental level, all humans are co-owners of this world, including its environment. What capitalism has unfortunately done is to unilaterally privatize the world, its resources and environment and eco-systems, so that these resources, eco-systems, and the environment actually belong to corporations and capitalists. Imperial domination has, in effect, turned Africans into sheer squatters on their own soil, unable to exercise decisive determination on the ownership and utilization of their resources. Dominated and exploited, Africans are laborers watching the destruction of their soils, their wildlife, and their environment under the direction of imperial economics. Hence, the theory of a caring capitalist economy, sensitive to protection of the environment, and an all- progressive imperial system, is an exercise in criminal deception.

III

The endemic question of racism against Africans (on the continent and in the diaspora) is deliberately omitted by the strategy of Half-Revolution. We cannot forget that from the advent of capitalism, the relationships between Africans and the West have been mediated through the prism of race and racism. From the days of the slave trade and slavery (which gave rise to capitalism), Africans (which of course includes Africans in the diaspora) have been victims of systematic and elaborate racism and bigotry. Theories have emerged to rationalize racism, including homicidal violence against us as a people. Racism is intricately woven into the economics of the slave trade, slavery, and capitalism. As a result, to accept subsistence under imperial domination is essentially to endorse our continued denigration as a people, since imperialism does not contain within it, mechanisms for our liberation. Capitalism and imperialism cannot eradicate racism against us on the continent and in the diaspora. Half-Revolution has no mechanism for addressing this question as a top priority for the regeneration of our cultures and our place in the world.

As part of our struggle for liberation, we must acknowledge that indeed our self- perception and the perception of our oppressors have been corrupted by our prolonged and tortured existence under imperialism. Aspects of the racist beliefs about us have seeped into our cultures and affected us in uncomfortable regressive ways. This has led to mental colonization. The manifestation of this defect, which leads to self-hatred, is the absorption and acceptance of the rationale for racism against us, a rationale formulated to fortify the slave trade, slavery, colonialism, and the unforgiveable exploitation of our labor. There are many Africans who continue to be affected by aspects of mental colonization, which includes self-hatred.

And since it is from the ranks of the educated that many revolutionary intellectuals are likely to be drawn, it is crucial to acknowledge and address the power of mental colonization. The aim is educational. The aim is to link this new effort to political and cultural education, and to view each correctly as an integral part of efforts toward the African revolution. The aim is not to blame, or to score individual victories, to finger point, or to engage in self-congratulation. No, not at all. That would be silly and counter -productive. All of us have been affected by aspects of cultural imperialism. The aim is to confront it and educate ourselves out of it as a deliberate effort in support of the African revolution.

In doing so, we recognize that it is very difficult for the oppressed to mentally liberate themselves in the absence of a properly articulated revolutionary ideology and purpose. For one thing, generations merge into one another. In other words, even if the new generation has a predisposition that is different from the previous one(s), this new generation is still physically and mentally linked to the receding generation. And as such, views, and opinions of the old find room in the new and they merge. Besides, the culture of the oppressor tends to be pervasive, influencing the behavior and consumption patterns of the oppressed. This reality underscores the educational and cultural value and inescapable necessity of the revolutionary party. The revolutionary elite cannot lead, cannot point to a new future, unless and until they have themselves purged this poison from their mental and cultural outlook and bearing. We cannot create a new tomorrow if, from the outset we have accepted that we are inferior to and less competent than our oppressors and exploiters.

Linked to this question of racism against us as Africans by the West is the rarely discussed matter of discriminations within the Global South. That is, even within groups routinely discriminated against by the West, you will find micro-levels of discrimination. And on a macro level, these large groups of people who have endured centuries of racism at the hands of the West find it acceptable to discriminate against one another.

There are those who will argue, with examples, that discrimination (micro and macro) has a long, tortured history and should be seen simply as an irrefutable part of human history and human nature, and that, if this is the case, we should not fret over it. For Africans on the continent and in the diaspora, we have good reason to determinedly fret over racism and discrimination. Modern racism against us is directly linked to the slave trade, slavery, and colonialism. On this point there can be very little dispute. Discrimination against us is linked to epochs in our history when we were most dominated, subdued, and exploited. Hence, discrimination against us is an external imposition; an elaborate system of rationalizations woven to justify our exploitation as labor.

Within the oppressed and the despised groups, communities, and even nationalities, there have formed pockets of power and privilege, giving rise to secondary enforcers of discrimination. Largely relying on the rationale fashioned by the slave traders, slave masters, and colonizers, groups and nations within the Global South declare themselves superior to this or that country, or this or that group. There is a jockeying for position among the despised. They seek to rise to the top in this category of the oppressed, victims of racism and discrimination. And here, they will go to the toolbox of slave traders, slave masters, colonizers, and empire builders for explanations and rationales. The key element in the distinction is simple: who is closest to the old master? Who now looks like the old master? Who resembles, in lifestyle and appearance, the old master? Who is the secondary old master, the local master of the despised? It is readily apparent that, in all of this exercise, efforts to categorize are wholly limited to within; in other words, the playbook stipulates that none of the despised groups can ever, ever, be equal to the West. The battle is for positions under the West.

And in keeping with dictates of the loaded history of the West on this question, discrimination against Africans, that is black people, is a common feature among many groups, even, on our continent, among groups who resist being identified as African. Here we see not only the residual power of the past, but, more specifically, the recurring impact of how we, in the Global South, were introduced to each other. Who introduced us, and what role did we have or play in this introduction? Who has guided our "knowing each other?" Who provides the details that we employ in assessing each other? Have we at all tried to deviate from the inherited script? What is the value of maintaining these levels of discrimination against each other?

In the absence of a progressive political ideology, relations among groups (and even nations) are profoundly influenced and directed by racism, prejudice, and discrimination, which continually fuel deliberate ignorance. Once such behaviors and attitudes are woven into local cultures, they become part of that society's foundational values. Let me provide some episodic illustration of this issue. A little while ago, I taught a young bright woman, originally from The Philippines. Her parents had migrated to the USA. In one of the many discussions in my course on "Pan-Africanism," we touched on the resiliency of racism against Africans, African Americans, and black people in general. Then I asked the non-white students (who were not African, African American, or of African heritage) if their communities discriminated against black people. The young lady from The Philippines volunteered that her community, her people, do discriminate against black people in general. In the USA, she had been instructed and then instructed again, by her parents and family not to marry a black man. They will allow her to marry a man from any race, but not a black man. Why so? Because, she said, black people are lazy, poor, violent, uncivilized, and prone to crime and drug use. How did her parents arrive at this? She did not really know. But they had been told this growing up and had also read about it since migrating to the USA and had seen it on TV and movies. On this question, it is fair to conclude that perpetuation of secondary discriminatory practices within the Global South works to advance imperial objectives. This equally applies to populations from the Global South who migrate and settle in the West.

Cultural imperialism, especially as it relates to self-hatred, has ensured that the oppressed look at each other through the binoculars provided by their imperial overlords. Thus, standards of beauty, integrity, pleasantness, attractiveness, mental abilities, desirability, and eligibility are all embraced, traced, and copied from the imperial manual—a dazzling display of cultural domination deemed sophistication. This self-hatred directs that the oppressed seek the embrace of the master. They do not really resent the master, the fountain of standards of beauty and sophistication. Even the most militant will, occasionally, reluctantly, sanction intermarriage with the master, but remain violently resistant to such intermarriage with groups in their country, and beyond, that are deemed inferior or undesirable. We must, therefore, acknowledge that this cultural domination of the master over supposedly free and independent peoples remains one of the most powerful weapons in the hands of the agents of imperialism.

Solidarity of the oppressed cannot emerge when the landscape is littered with prejudices, hatreds, and inclinations to emulate the master in their efforts to categorize one another. Solidarity of the oppressed and the despised cannot emerge when all of our energies are geared toward catching the eye of the master. All those non-whites who rightfully rail against white racism must oppose discrimination and prejudice at every turn, including in their own communities and countries. If you oppose discrimination, then stand up against it everywhere, including in your own country and community. There is no tolerable discrimination, there is no justifiable discrimination or prejudice against a people as dictated by culture, tradition, or bogus biological essentialism. The strategy of Half-Revolution lacks the ideological framework to reach this crucial conclusion.

The struggle for liberation is firmly based on the principle of equality. This principle espouses the following non-negotiable details: racial equality, gender equality, and social equality of all peoples. We cannot fight for equality while endorsing and affirming sectional superiority of any kind. The quest for liberation becomes a shameful fraud the moment we insist on our own sectional superiority. If, as established, imperialism is the enemy, then we must resist, by all means, any attempts to emulate the strategies and inclinations of the master. Self-hatred and the pursuit of sectional superiority under imperialism, exist in all dominated minds, homes, and peoples.

REVOLUTION THIS TIME: A THEORY OF AFRICAN REVOLUTION

I

The question of self-definition is absolutely crucial to any society engaged in national revolutionary struggle. The starting point in such struggle is that the formulation of a national revolutionary ideology is an attempt at self-definition. This partly explains the repeated failure of neo-colonialism in the Global South. Can it really be imagined that, in an attempt to define themselves, Africans opt to be oppressed, exploited, and denigrated? Neo-colonial regimes fail because they are a fraud, a dangerous oppressive fraud. Neo-colonial regimes also seek to attain the impossible: to turn imperialism into an ideology of liberation.

The deeper meaning of neo-colonialism is that the dominated countries are denied an opportunity to define themselves. The dominated are defined and labelled by others. The dominated country is treated by imperialism as a perpetually ignorant (and occasionally petulant) child, whose growth is guided by the master and therefore subject to repeated corrective discipline.

After more than fifty years of *Uhuru* (political freedom) for many countries in Africa, the majority of our people are still poor, oppressed, exploited, and manipulated. The ruling elite have abused their power on a regular basis and have ruled and behaved like local viceroys, like local governors of an external power. It has been painfully evident that the ruling elite have not even been nationalistic in their objectives, method, tendencies, or projections. They are greedy, selfish, and short-sighted. The ruling elite have squandered national wealth by stealing it and storing it overseas. They do not even trust the viability of the countries they rule and loot from. They are in power to steal and plunder, not to liberate and develop.

The ruling elite have no regard or respect for the people, the citizens. They despise the local populations. Thus, they despise their fellow Africans while they respect and honor their external imperial masters.

On a regular basis, the ruling elite have demonstrated that they do not respect the most elementary stipulations of democratic rule and so, with shameless impunity, they "steal elections," manipulate the electoral process, bribe, and kill, in order to retain power.

In reality, the ruling elite in Africa have accepted their roles as collaborators, as facilitators of the imperial mission. They will, therefore, never challenge this imperial overlordship on behalf of their home countries and their home continent. Such a challenge is not their burning objective while in power. They hang on the "sacredness of current territorial integrity" in order to exercise monopoly over local power, which facilitates their thieving habits and indulgence. To this end, they have installed institutions and agencies, led by trusted loyalists, that protect their wealth and choke to death any would-be challengers. The people, the masses are permanently locked out of the house. There is no way of gaining entry except by overthrowing the ruling elite. There is no way to end this oppressive and exploitative rule except to overthrow it.

The coming African revolution, a people's revolt against imperialism, will advance these aims and objectives: a struggle against external imperial economic, social, and political domination; a determined drive toward social justice and equality and therefore a struggle against local and external oppression; the establishment of policies and programs that embrace and advance gender and sexual equality in all forms; the banning of racism, racist bigotry, and any allusions to preferences based on race; a fervent adherence to and propagation of Pan-African solidarity as the cornerstone of all external policies; the resistance to and thwarting of any tendencies toward internal discrimination and local dictatorship; the establishment of a national identity based on a vibrant progressive ideology and corresponding resistance toward any ethnic jingoism or "tribal triumphalism"; the establishment of a strong national economy with durable Pan-African connections; and the expansion of credible institutions of learning to educate local populations and supply local expertise.

The path of subsisting and surviving under imperialism is, in essence, driving a rickety vehicle at a slow, painful speed toward a cul-de-sac. There is no outlet, there has never been an outlet, for our development, integrity, and cultural renewal. All those determined to bring into being the African revolution this time must, from the onset, be resistant to the seductive power of imperialism and its hollow shimmering mirage of promises. Can we afford to be seduced again and again by the false promises of development under the guidance of imperialism? The visible results of this paralyzing seduction have been our permanent poverty, the denial of life and happiness to our people, and then our relegation to the perpetual denigrating status of beggars, facilitators, and collaborators.

The building and sustaining of revolution in Africa now, is predicated upon a thorough and detailed criticism of imperialism. On this issue, the clearly stated position is that imperialism is the enemy. Thus, the values that will underpin this African revolution will be based entirely on socialism in pursuit of communism. The unalterable aim is for Africa to cut forever its long enduring subordinate status under the Western yoke. In our analysis of imperial plunder and oppression, we must always remember that, if done properly, our conclusions will differ markedly from those of Western liberal scholars. We occupy different positions on the ladder of power. Our encounter with Western institutions is different. Our vision is different. And as we rise, they fall. All of this is self-evident and logical.

Any revolutionary movement in Africa will be immediately faced with the task of swimming against the current of deep seated and well-organized propaganda.

This propaganda is deep rooted in schools, in the political arena, in the academic world, in business and industry, in the media and book world—all strenuously opposed to revolution, socialism, and communism. Since the dissolution of the Soviet Union in 1991, these propaganda outlets have embarked on a journey of mischief with no hurdles or obstacles in sight. Look at how many books and articles have been published to reinforce the essence of preexisting propaganda positions against socialism and communism. These are not new revelations at all. They are old tales given new varnish and accompanying footnotes by an ever-expanding list of "experts, scholars and authorities." The end product, the desired outcome, has remained the same as before: Fear communism. Never embrace communism or socialism. Communism is bad. Communism is the enemy. All of these overt and covert propaganda offensives against communism have been principally linked to the Russian revolution.

The study of the Russian revolution (and indeed, other post– World War II Marxist revolutions in the Global South) constitutes one of the most shameful episodes in Western scholarship. For all the degrees earned and the honors dished out and the Fellowships created, the Russian revolution remains an enigma in the West for the simple reason that the West has not sought to understand it. Rather, the consistent uninterrupted objective has been to condemn and damn the revolution. Nor should we forget that the rise of Russian Studies in the USA was fundamentally a CIA project. The CIA did not sponsor this project in the initial stages in order to produce information that celebrated the Russian revolution. (See: Noam Chomsky, et al.,

The Cold War &The University, New York: The New Press, 1997 and Frances Stonor Saunders, *The Cultural Cold War: The CIA and the World of Arts and Letters*, New York: The New Press, 1999.) There is no evidence suggesting any subsequent forthright deviation from this original intent which sought to resolutely discredit the ideological underpinnings of communism and especially its operational details in the Soviet Union. Here was an inherently defective ideology whose leaders were partly mentally deranged and certainly deceitful power-hungry thugs. The followers were portrayed as people apart, easily manipulated, and products of cultural traditions that tolerated dictatorships and abuse of power. Those followers fought for what they did not understand and could never understand. For, who, in their right mind, could ever voluntarily support communism unless they were simpletons or deceived or forced to do so through unrelenting terror? This is Western cultural arrogance and bias framed as rational analysis of historical events.

The rest of the world, especially in the Global South, was introduced to communism and the Russian revolution (and other post–World War II revolutions) through the elaborate anti-communist writings issuing from Western scholars, newspapers, entertainment industry, TV, the church, education, broadcasts, journals, periodicals, magazines, books, and official propaganda that was elevated and labelled as objective analysis. For the last one hundred years, the rest of the world has been held captive to Western propaganda in all guises and shapes. What we know, what we purport to know, is gleaned through the Western prism. We are invited as guests (of varied importance) to witness the screening of a finished film. Whatever our muffled comments may be, the truth is that these efforts cannot alter the shape and details of the finished film. Indeed, the hosts are dismayed that we can even dare raise questions. We may write a few comments here and there, but these are easily dismissed, usually derisively.

The impact of one hundred years of continuous propaganda against the Russian revolution and communism has left in its wake impressive results. Perhaps the most disheartening has been the creation in the West of layers upon layers of lazy scholarship. That scholarship starts with a given and well-established conclusion—that communism is horrible, deceitful, oppressive, and reprehensible. This is a conclusion in line with the objectives of the Western intelligence agencies since 1917. It is an old song, just sung by different generations of musicians. Now, it has become sacred. The lyrics and even the accompanying music are seen as a sacred classic. And, of course, Western scholars dare not attempt to tinker with this classic. It does not trouble them that their many books and conference proceedings in the end resemble official tracts and conclusions. In other words, this is the basic definition of co-opted scholarship, which still looks at itself as grand and objective.

These scholars and journalists and other "authorities" know their audience who buy their books, read their tracts, and listen to them on TV and radio and other outlets. It is a well-cultivated audience, an audience with a deliberately established and now well-known mindset. This audience is expecting even more lurid details about the misdeeds of communist governments, especially in the Soviet Union under Stalin. And so, however new the books may be, they are in reality very old. These authors seek to be heard, to be read, and then elevated in their positions. They cannot attain these distinctions by swimming against the current. To be sure, they can distinguish themselves by seeming more sophisticated in analysis, more reasoned, better sourced, and more measured and nuanced, but in the end their contributions are not in essence very different from the crude and unscholarly voices. In both cases, the authors and speakers count on a deep and well cultivated anti-communism prevalent in their society. Their books and tracts reinforce this disposition.

Complaints about university students, at least in the USA, that they do not read beyond prescribed texts may be well founded. But, in many cases, the society and even their teachers, do not really want them to wander off into unsanctioned directions and areas of inquiry. They are expected to read the assigned and recommended texts in order to arrive at a preexisting grand conclusion: that the West and its values and institutions are close to being infallible. A study in incomparable achievement. Deeply held anti-communist propaganda in the society has established this position as absolute and therefore not subject to rational contradiction. And so, for all the exhortations encouraging students to think creatively and to be original, this is not a sincere wish or claim, and the students know it. Students can read prescribed and suggested texts with the understanding that they will come back to the established idea that communism is evil and must be fought and vanquished. What is truly encouraged is for these students to find new and better ways of enhancing the glory and performance of capitalism and imperialism, a search for new and profitable ways of reinforcing the status quo. And also, to rejoice in the fact that they live in the West and are part of the Western tradition. The imperial component of this tradition (past and present) is avoided. When mentioned (if at all), the majority of the emphasis is on its "positive contributions to world history and development." Whenever Western scholars and politicians engage in rousing songs of praise about capitalism and imperialism, they deliberately skip over inconvenient revealing details. The West is very good at this sort of thing: strategic evasion and the forthright and determined dismissal of contradictory evidence.

During the Cold War, the West came to characterize communism as "the god that failed." (See: Arthur Koestler, *The God that Failed*, New York: Harper & Brothers, 1949.) Communism was portrayed as deceptive, a crude manipulation of human sentiments, and impossible to implement given what the West saw as the basics of human nature. This verdict was, of course, meant to scare would-be sympathizers, to warn them of the inevitable cruel disappointment that they will endure should they opt to follow the path of the "Godless Reds." Communism was dictatorship and oppression and the end of freedom. Alongside other propaganda outlays, these characterizations sought to point to all the dominated classes and peoples in terms of how lucky they were to be living under Western imperialism. The oppressed and the exploited were informed that in fact they were free. They had to avoid communism since it is a conspiracy against hard work, it encourages laziness and lack of personal advancement, and, yes, it is anti-family. In more crude forms, communism was rumored to favor the sharing of wives. How could they support such an ideology?

If communism is "the god that failed," what should be said of capitalism and imperialism? How many times in one day does capitalism fail in its declared mission to be the engine of worldwide development? A cursory look shows that capitalism is the god that never walked, especially in the Global South. Here is a god prone to endless economic recessions, a god that promises more than it can deliver. Here is a god that endorses and tolerates discrimination and racism, oppression and shameless exploitation. A god that has, for centuries, tragically failed again and again to provide food, shelter, and education to billions of people under its domination. This is a god that revels in greed and essentially sees no hope in sight for billions of people who are nonetheless expected to show their gratitude for living in poverty under capitalism. Endless poverty and endless exploitation. A god that aggressively destroys the environment in pursuit of profits.

Perhaps more revealing is the indisputable fact that this god of capitalism has failed even without competition. To fail to succeed, to deliver on its promises and claims in the face of no competition whatsoever is the clearest evidence yet of the inherent fallacy of capitalism's posturing as the savior of humankind. It is a god destined to fail every day in spite of its lofty claims. This failure is world-wide in scope; it cannot be hidden or blamed on the mischief of a rival ideology. Poverty cannot be hidden. Poor housing cannot be hidden. Poor schools and lack of medical care cannot be hidden. Environmental destruction cannot be hidden. Reliance on brutality (police and other security agencies) to enforce obedience and secure the status quo exposes the ravenous and gangster nature of the system. Racism cannot be hidden. And there is no possible rationale that can be readily employed to explain away these several failures by capitalism. No belligerent conduct can, in the long run, be readily employed to safeguard the system. Hence, more resort to force and brutality and intolerance. The system is nonetheless teetering, swaying in the wind of historical forces. The barrel has started to roll down the cliff.

A strategy increasingly employed in the West, and specifically in the USA, is to announce without apology, that even if capitalism has problems, it is the only system on the table; that it is the only system still standing. This cynical declaration is always couched in arrogant, dismissive, and abrasive terms. It is the equivalent of "take it or leave it." But these arrogant postures, born in fear and deep-seated insecurity about the future, do not in themselves provide a coherent explanation as to why capitalism is unable to deliver at its supposedly most triumphant moment. There is no organized resistance to capitalism at this period. All governments have capitulated. It has ensured that its rationale for existence in its current form is forcefully accepted by all governments. And of course, its cultural presumptions and values dominate the airwaves and publications and screens. The bulk of published literature, books, and articles are critical of communism. Yet, in spite of all these overwhelming advantages (and power), capitalism has failed to deliver. It has failed to win in what is really a one-person competition. That is the very definition of failure.

The West (under capitalism and imperialism) believes in self-delusion about its own inherent greatness, the miracle of its formation and existence. Miraculously, the West arose owing nothing, if at all, to Africa. The West, all so very industrious, hardworking, inventive, all so ingenious, all so far-sighted, all so disciplined and frugal. This is self-delusion, but it underpins the West's image of itself. Through colonialism, neo-colonialism, and general cultural domination, Africans have been forced by the West to see merit in this delusion, even if it means using readily supplied super-magnifying glasses and skipping over several crucial pages in the glossy pictorial. In formulating and then projecting this self-delusion, the West denies the very existence of imperialism, past and present. As part of this African revolution, we Africans, must expose the nature of the true West to ourselves and then to the West itself. In this way, we shall liberate the West from this beguiling self-delusion.

A crucial detail in the drive toward the African revolution is to acknowledge that the majority of the key successful revolutionary movements in the post-1917 period, waged in the name of the people, have all had some allegiance to socialism and communism. While the details have differed, the product of geography, history, culture, and initial circumstances, the preeminent successful revolutionary movements have been waged in the name of the people under the banner of socialism and communism. These revolutionary movements have been launched to dethrone and oust imperial domination and create a non-oppressive, non-racist, and non-exploitative system.

What has been made self-evident by history is that people fight for dignity, equality, social justice, and against racism, exploitation, oppression, sexism, and all forms of discrimination. For people to sacrifice they have to be assured that tomorrow will lead to advancements in their lives—that there will be improvements in their economic prospects; that their children will have a future; that, as a people, they will be respected; and that women will secure equal status; that they will stop living in fear. Under imperialism we are despised, humiliated, disrespected, undervalued, exploited, and oppressed natives. There is no historical evidence to contradict this painful reality.

II

Can there be an "indigenous ideology" that is anti-imperialist but not socialist? Do we have local ideologies that are not socialist but resolutely opposed to Western imperialism, that contain within them mechanisms for radically implementing equality and social justice? That promote, as their basic defining characteristics, opposition to: discrimination, oppression, exploitation, and racial hierarchy; that promote equality, social justice, and fervently endorse and promote gender and sexual equality; and that strive for international peace based on equality of peoples and nations?

In the Global South, poverty, misrule, and deprivations of the past and the present have led to the formation of multiple local movements of resistance against local centers. Some of these movements have scored momentary lightning success. But they ultimately falter. The problem has to do with their essential goal; the declared vision, if any, of the society. A liberation movement is destined to fail if it embraces or tolerates terror, oppression, and exploitation, for then it quickly ceases to be the focus of liberation. Hence, a liberation movement cannot be seen to assume the tactics of the imperial enemy—brutal, intolerant, sadistic, callous, discriminatory, racist, sexist, etc. These are tested weapons of the imperial enemy. They must not be allowed as the favored tactics in the fight *against* the imperial enemy. And we must concede that, while fear and terror can hold a people, a population, to a resistance movement for a brief period, they cannot sustain the growth and expansion of a liberation movement.

It is, therefore, erroneous to imagine that fear plus terror can lead to conquest against imperialism. This is the strategy of militarism that has been exposed by history to be misguided and ineffective in any meaningful struggle against imperialism. The failure of militarism lies in its lack of connection to the people through the political process expounding on its life-giving aims and objectives. Fear and terror can have the power of initial shock. But after some time, fear ceases to induce awe. It breeds resistance, and this resistance can be easily exploited by the agents of imperialism. Also, fear does not respect and advance the overriding political, cultural, economic justification for the struggle. Explosions of terror against potential recruits and their families denies it audience, leading to more brutality and more resistance. Are those who are held in fear enemies or supporters of the movement? Will those held in fear convert to support the "new cause" if the present is deemed more frightening and oppressive than the past?

In the long run, the fight or resistance in the name of local ideology can only succeed against imperialism if what it promises is better than the past and the present: if its program of action exemplifies commitment to equality and social justice. And, also, if it is guided by these words from Amilcar Cabral: "Always bear in mind that the people are not fighting for ideas, for things in any one's head. People fight and they accept the necessary sacrifices in order to win material benefits, to live better and in peace, to see their lives go forward, and to guarantee the future of their children." (Amilcar Cabral, *Revolution in Guinea: Selected Texts*, New York: Monthly Review Press, 1969: 86.) This is the eternal guiding principle. It is hence inconceivable that any local resistance movement can achieve these essential goals unless it is guided by a deep abiding commitment to social justice, socialism, and communism. The vision of the future must demonstrate now, during the struggle, that tomorrow will resist abrasive abuse of power; that it will foster equality, and banish oppression, sexism, racism, discrimination, exploitation, and other maladies associated with imperialism.

The struggle toward the African revolution will be forced to encounter and then overcome the poison that is ethnic nationalism, or "tribalism," as the West revels in identifying these identities and tendencies in modern Africa. The politics and economics of colonialism, and now neo-colonialism, have succeeded in converting these identities into super-charged and coiled political forces. On occasion, they have turned into unspeakably horrific murderous eruptions. Nothing has caused more damage, delayed national cohesion, led to homicides and even genocides, as this modern curse. We can all agree that this reality of modern ethnic antagonism is the creation of imperialism. In its current form, now made even more rigid and unyielding in its obsessions, ethnic nationalism has been given new life, new corrosive life, by the misdeeds of the neo-colonial regimes. The urge for Africans to define themselves in these terms is, in itself, a clear illustration of the failure of the center and the need for a national progressive ideology.

Devoid of any progressive national focus and agenda, neo-colonialism courts and promotes "tribalism." Regrettably, the ruling elite have seized on these several ethnic nationalisms as a base of power struggle on the national stage. What they seek is power to subdue in order to exploit. They seek to "tribalize" national politics and thereby nullify the relevance and importance of a rigorous class analysis of these countries. A progressive ideology can only emerge from a class analysis of these societies. What they seek is to be well remunerated executioners of the imperial agenda. What they seek is to postpone to infinity the sacred project of nation building in the name of the people. What they seek is to confuse the masses about the causes of their poverty and powerlessness, by misdirecting this anger away from them to invented "enemies from other tribes." We have to look at the ruling elite and all those learned intellectuals in Africa who subscribe to "tribalism" as enemies of the people, enemies of nation-building.

The difficult task of nation-building in Africa has been side-stepped in favor of power struggle among the ruling elite under the guise of "tribal politics." In this matter, we seem to have accepted the imperial thesis which postulates that indeed we cannot live together under one roof because of "tribalism." The difficult yet crucial matter of institutional building to support national cohesion has been abandoned. In its place, we have improvised policy making, without coherence, whose results inevitably fail to advance national cohesion or development. The business of politics has become a quest for avenues and opportunities to facilitate looting, stealing, and robbing and then framing all these nefarious activities as national development. The result is that we are feverishly walking in a circle and strangely referring to this activity as forward movement, as national development. Ethnic nationalism must, therefore, be seen as a clear and present danger to any credible efforts aimed at nation-building and cohesion in Africa.

To be clear, the African revolution will respect and rejoice in the rich tapestry of African cultures and languages. The current real threat to the very existence of these cultures and their values is from the flattening power of globalization, that is, imperialism.

The African revolution shall neither seek nor advocate for the eradication of African ethnic groups/entities/nationalities and their cultures. We all benefit from the presence of this rich tapestry. But this is different, and must be considered differently, from using these cultural variations (and even differences) as an historic justification for a claim to power, for an ascent to power, for holding onto power, or for looting and sanctioning of oppression and exploitation. We can rejoice in this tapestry without making an indefensible leap toward entitlement that inevitably produces "tribal hegemony and dictatorship." Such dictatorship has on occasion been tragically accompanied by resort to "biological essentialism," which invokes bogus biology and science to justify domination and oppression. The dominant "tribe" assumes some inherent indescribable superiority and attributes found lacking in other "tribes." The urge to invoke bogus biology and other indefensible attributes poisons the well, while also preparing the ground for ethnic violent eruptions.

In the absence of a progressive national ideology, the drive to attain top positions is essentially a scramble for keys to the central bank, access to subsidiaries of multinational corporations, the banking sector, national assets, and government offices that can facilitate thievery and bribery. The lure of "tribalism" is to secure and advance the economic and political ambitions of chiefs, royalties, "tribal dignitaries," coalitions of "big men," criminals, and warlords. The ugly net result has been endless quarrels that rise to become charged national crises. This formula represents a glistening dead end. It pulls our energies into a state of constant tension. It limits our political imagination and formulation. It legitimizes theft, trickery, oppression, and exploitation. It is afraid of unity and progressive ideas, let alone revolution.

A poisonous relic of colonialism was the introduction of ethnic-based political parties and "tribal leaders." In subsequent periods, the political orientations in most countries have been shaped by appeals to ethnic loyalty as opposed to a non-ethnic political formulation/party. No amount of education or academic qualifications have been able to erase this blinding loyalty. And on cue, every conceivable "scholarly argument" is adduced to explain, justify, and affirm this disabling orientation. Under this scheme, loyalty is regional, ethnic, and these are rigid and charged. As it relates to national politics, such loyalties invariably tolerate and even endorse class divisions within the group. Oppression and exploitation within the group are tolerated and explained away. Academic tracts, in one form or another, can be easily produced to affirm this "tribal distinction and uniqueness" and therefore justification to wealth and power. Ethnic identity is summoned to demand unbending and unconditional loyalty to social and class divisions within the unit/region. You are loyal to the extent that you endorse internal oppression and exploitation. You are expected to continually smile in the face of all these contradictions. All for your "tribe."

Nation-building in Africa must disavow, denounce, and repudiate ethnic nationalism, regional nationalism, and similar orientations, once they become, as they always do, spring- boards for domination, oppression, and exploitation: once they become pillars of resistance toward national cohesion. We know that communities and groups have been continually disadvantaged, looted, exploited, and oppressed. We also know that scholarly justifications have been found to endorse this national shame.

There can be no African revolution without deliberate re-orientation of national politics from ethnic to national, from regional to national, from dynastic rule to a national progressive ideology based on class, the result of a detailed class analysis of our countries and societies. There is an urgent compelling need to move away from dead-end localized, ethnic, or regional loyalty to a progressive national agenda dedicated to equality and social justice. Ethnic or regional yearning for supremacy is of necessity regressive and, in the end, unworkable. To enforce it, a section of well-connected individuals or families, speaking in the name of the "tribe" or region, must seize power and then scheme to hold onto it in perpetuity by force. Thus, inherent in ethnic nationalism and regional loyalty is a compulsory embrace of terror, oppression, and exploitation. No bridge exists, under neocolonial conditions, that links ethnic nationalism to national cohesion and purpose. Ethnic nationalism cannot be a force of national liberation. Hence, conceptually, and functionally, you cannot be a "tribalist" and a socialist. The formula of "tribalism" cannot be democratic, nor can it seriously advance social justice and resistance against imperial plunder. It does not provide a road map toward national cohesion or national integration.

No ideology or political program based on or linked to capitalism and imperial greed can provide a framework for overcoming the heated and charged matter of ethnic nationalism as a pressing national problem in Africa. Indeed, the existence of ethnic (and even racial) divide advances the imperial agenda: divide and conquer. In this way, we fight over peripheral details, while leaving imperialism undisturbed in our countries. Capitalism, and its laden contradictions, has been unable to provide a credible framework for overcoming ethnic nationalism, regional disputes, racial tension, and racism, and other social forces that conspire against national cohesion and solidarity. Capitalism has no formula, theoretical or otherwise, for nullifying the already charged forces of ethnic nationalism and racism.

How about the law? Can resort to court battles undermine and even overthrow the neo-colonial regimes and usher in the African revolution? Can the law and the courts save Africa and facilitate the installation of radical revolutionary governments and systems? Part of the tragedy of post-*Uhuru* Africa is the proliferation of rulers (and their governments) who lack the ability to accept responsibility, to concede, to be ashamed. Impunity grows and thrives in societies where the rulers can no longer be ashamed of their deeds. Impunity erases humility and produces leaders who refuse, with open contempt, to accept responsibility for their misdeeds. Impunity ensures that rulers hold their positions in contravention of law and legal provisions that are routinely brushed aside or amended to suit the desires of the powerful. Such leaders effectively rule like the old colonial governors: repressive and indifferent to the wishes of their subjects.

The strategy of resisting terror and exploitation through the legal system alone has not yielded a sterling record of victories in Africa. There was thus an understandable joy and jubilation across Africa in September 2017, when the Supreme Court in Kenya overturned a presidential election. Chief Justice Maraga and his colleagues on the Supreme Court issued a majority ruling which determined that indeed the national presidential election held in August 2017 was fatally compromised. It was messy, irregular, and illegal on many counts. In this ruling, the Supreme Court sided with the primary arguments of the political coalition National Super Alliance: that indeed the election had been conducted in an illegal manner marred by numerous glaring irregularities. The totality of the votes repeatedly cited by President Uhuru Kenyatta's Jubilee Party were found to have been the fruit of illegal criminal activities. What the Supreme Court determined was that numbers or votes cannot stand alone independent of the process that produced them. The numbers must be viewed against the backdrop of the process. How were the numbers generated? How were the numbers transmitted and tabulated? Thus, illegally attained numbers cannot and should not be accepted or acknowledged as a basis for electoral victory.

Chief Justice Maraga struck at the nerve center of the electoral corruption prevalent in many countries in Africa and beyond. Politicians have been able to manipulate the process by controlling the final tally, which renders voting an exercise in expensive futility. Those who count the votes control the outcome. The Supreme Court ruled that you cannot contravene the law and then benefit from your illegal and criminal activities. And that, at all times, the process must be transparent, verifiable, and consistent. From a historical perspective, this ruling marks the first time that a presidential election (of an incumbent president) has been nullified in Africa. We do not have many examples elsewhere. It is therefore historic in form and dimension.

Yet this act of courage on the part of Chief Justice Maraga's court did not, in itself, overthrow abuse of power in the country nor signal the end of neo-colonialism and foreign domination of the national economy. The euphoria that accompanied this historic decision soon evaporated as the ruling elite reasserted their hold on the major pillars of power: the administrative machinery, the police, the army, the banking industry, and access to national assets. The unprecedented ruling by the Supreme Court was a specific corrective legal remedy affecting one national institution, the Independent Electoral and Boundaries Commission and its mishandling of the national elections in August 2017. By this one decision, the Supreme Court did not presume to morph into the people's national liberation front. It would, therefore, be a tactical error to rely on courts to liberate the country from oppression and exploitation and from the fangs of imperialism. The judiciary cannot, through its rulings, institute a different national political system. Courts, even under the best of circumstances, do not write the laws that they are then called upon to uphold and interpret within the context of the national constitution. They function within a prescribed political system with, hopefully, well-articulated values and principles. And even the power of the courts is very much affected by the operative political climate. The enforcement of their rulings is dependent upon the administrative machinery invariably controlled by the national political system. Power to enforce is always political. A corrupt and vicious ruling elite can ignore court rulings and even arrest the offending judges.

Both the power and limitations of courts to advance the semblance of social justice is open for all to see in the USA. Appointments to the US Supreme Court have always been a political matter. Rulings by this court determine how US citizens interact as a people: their safety; where they can live and work; how much control they have over their person and body; where they can eat or drink; where they can go to school; what banks and companies can do; what rights, including voting rights, can be protected; the place of money in politics, etc. It is about power.

It is about seizing power and tilting it in specific directions. It is about the multiple definitions of justice. A study of the rulings of the Supreme Court brings you closer to comprehending and appreciating the varied historical currents that have flowed and continue to flow through the US political system and social structure. Such a study also allows you to see the power of the class and racial structures and their imprint on the definition(s) of justice and legal rights.

Power and powerlessness fuels societal struggles over appointments of judges to the US Supreme Court. At the moment, in the first two decades of the 21st century, the majority of the US population feel all too powerless to have any direct influence on the course of events in their country. In spite of the soothing propaganda shouted from the rooftops, proclaiming the people are in-charge of their destinies, the reality is that the majority of the citizens are unable to cause direct drastic changes in and on national institutions of power; to make these institutions responsive to the poor, the powerless, the disadvantaged. There can be no true social justice without fundamentally revising or eliminating the laws that protect the rich and the powerful against the fundamental interests of the poor and those living on the margins of society.

There is, nonetheless, an abiding residual faith in the power of courts to render corrective judgements. The belief, repeatedly abused, is that courts can bring to an end any excessive abuse of power and authority; that courts can render impartial justice, indifferent to race, class, gender, sex, status, etc. In the absence of any other alternatives, the courts have come to be seen as the last weapon available against injustice and abuse of power. The fear within the country is that the current conservative majority on the Supreme Court (as of 2021) will remain unapologetic in their political bias in favor of the rich and the powerful and against the poor, the disadvantaged, women, etc. The court has in its recent rulings provided legal rationalizations for abuse of power, greed, racism, sexism, discrimination, etc. What we have here is the gates being closed to any, and all, pretenses toward social justice.

The anguish of the powerless over these appointments is a strong indicator of their social vulnerability. It also provides us with a window into their chronic insecurity: living in a society that scorns their poverty and weakness and laughs at them and their powerlessness. A liberal leaning court may seek to curb, somewhat, the egregious excesses of power, privilege, and bigotry and gently open the door to social justice a few inches wider.

Currently in the USA, and indeed in all those countries supportive of Western imperialism, the ruling elite see no need for such pretenses. They seek to hold onto power more solidly, flaunt their wealth and power, and drive the striving masses to their proper place: at the bottom, with no voice. Now that there is no Cold War, there is no need to be apologetic about white supremacy, racism, power, bigotry, sexism, classes, and greed. Let capitalism dance. Let imperialism dance.

The rich and the powerful always overreach. They are not satisfied with just oppressing and exploiting the majority. The rich have a compelling need and urge to make the poor endlessly remember their powerlessness. Inherent in oppression and exploitation is a perpetual hunger for sadism, a thirst for the blood of the weak. The rich do not feel powerful until and unless such blood is flowing. To cause harm (social, political, and economic) and then not be held accountable at all, constitutes one of the unspoken but well-known perks of power and privilege. The courts are, in theory, supposed to stand on the side of the powerless, to protect them.

This belief is reinforced by occasional victories in the courts against, for example, overt racial segregation in sports, education, housing, etc. And these victories seem to suggest that indeed you can wrestle down discrimination and injustice through the courts. But these victories are few and far between; haphazard. They also tend to be specific and constrained. Through legal interpretation, aspects of such victories may be extended to other areas of society affected by similar or related issues. The reliance on court victories alone also sidesteps the need for systematic organization. Macro movements are routinely avoided so long as it is imagined that that the courts will act as restraints on extremism.

Fundamentally, however, these victories cannot, and must not, be seen as a conspiracy against the basic structure and values of the system. As it happens, these rulings reinforce the system. This is important. By seeming to provide hope, these rulings discourage radical analysis and appraisal of the system; they frown upon radical solutions to deep-rooted social problems. They incline toward foraging for solutions in the magical coils of the system. Even in those areas of deep-seated racism, for example, there are no identifiable linear efforts toward eradication of this social evil. Forward movement is never secure; there is the ever-present fear of reversal. There has never been a wholesale collective effort toward the enforcement of the laws on the books regarding discrimination and racism. Loopholes have been found to dilute and then downgrade expected consequences. The reality is that there has never been a societal commitment to end discrimination and racism in the USA. And you notice very quickly that the white populations immediately launch what can be termed a kind of guerilla warfare against any, and all, rulings linked to the quest for racial equality and social justice. This includes Affirmative Action programs. There is an immediate denunciation of such rulings. There has never been a ruling by the Supreme Court to advance racial equality that has been greeted by dancing and celebration in the streets of white America. We do not have examples or instances of white populations dancing, rejoicing, and euphorically hailing those rulings of the Supreme Court that seemed to promise forward positive movement toward racial equality and an end to discrimination. One can argue that, in fact, racial equality has come to be seen as essentially un-American: not part of the country's defining values and principles. For all the talk on public platforms and in writings about the search for racial equality, the American way, and the values contained in the Declaration of Independence, the Bill of Rights, etc., the constant reality has been that whites in the USA have repeatedly recoiled in resistance and horror at the very mention or thought of consequential racial equality.

The rulings of the courts, always dependent on the political alignment of the judges, even if occasionally in favor of the poor and disadvantaged on a limited basis, tend to be overtaken by events and history. And after some time, due to resistance against the rulings and many revisions, the expected positive results dwindle and evaporate. The system that produces the injustices remains in place.

How about political reforms? Can we rely on political reforms to deal a death blow to neo-colonialism—and all of its social baggage—in Africa? Can neo-colonialism be reformed out of existence in Africa? Are political reforms the most effective strategy in the fight against imperialism? The history of postcolonial Africa does not provide much hope for this strategy. Like colonial rule, neo-colonial oppressive governments and ruling elites have continually demonstrated their singular inability to reform, to adopt effective democratic reforms. These regimes have been intolerant of calls for reforms and have understood that to reform is (for them) to die, that adoption of concrete democratic reforms inevitably leads to their loss of power.

Reliance on brutal force, cults of personality, "indispensable rulers," and their decrees provides no room for reforms. Neocolonial regimes live in perpetual fear of their subjects and also are aware of the naked fact that they are illegitimate impostors. They lack the ability to be creative, or even nationalistic. They cannot, therefore, be anti-imperialistic, for imperialism is, after all, the basis of their existence. The result is rigidity and terror against their subjects. They are adept at looting but not at nation building; they know how to divide, but not how to unite and chart new paths forward for national development. While they insist on a formula that has worked for them, they have no answer to the question of inclusive, cohesive, and egalitarian nation building. Greed and loyalty to their imperial masters have left these regimes with a minimum of political courage and imagination. On some level, these regimes must be considered local foreign rulers. And they must be treated as such: as foreign rulers and looters. Hence, the African revolution is a people's effort to attain their liberation from these local foreign rulers and, along with it, their dignity.

It is still nonetheless necessary to inquire as to how any trust in reforms can undermine and dislodge capitalism, let alone neocolonialism and its imperial hold on the country. Examples from the West, specifically the USA, indicate that agitation for reforms, even when those reforms are partially attained, does not make the system shake at its foundations. The fundamental shape and aims of the system are not undermined, despite the system's allowing certain reforms. Most of the energy of the fractious progressive movements in the USA has been directed at organizing for small incremental changes at the local, county level, and only occasionally at the state and federal level. This has, from time to time, involved petitioning the courts for redress. But these efforts have been haphazard, not continuous; ad hoc in nature and lacking in systematic organization. Under such circumstances, it is difficult to measure progress to any real degree. This is the true example of unequal development on many social levels. How then can we measure progress, and what does progress mean here? Where does the next generation pick up? Will the next generation pick up the same fight or a new one? There has also been a drift toward individualized progressivism. And some of it has been, as expected, very peculiar and idiosyncratic. But does the totality of these individualized, uneven, haphazard efforts constitute a forward march toward liberation?

Multiplicity of movements—many, small and isolated—gives rise to multiple meanings of these efforts and desired outcomes. On a macro level (even on a micro level), what does progressivism mean here? Do progressives in the USA imagine a more humane capitalist society as the preferred outcome of their efforts? Would such a society still be imperialist? Is the aim here to reform capitalism or dismantle it? Can mild reforms in themselves create a different economic and social system? Further, is it realistic to imagine that in fact there can be a non-exploitative, non-imperialist capitalist society? What is the inspiration for such imagination among these progressives?

The progressives in the West will continue to confront the contradiction of looking for change in no change; to face the fact of their remaining essentially passive and hoping and wishing that time, and time alone, will deliver some form of radical change to their doorstep; hoping that inevitable societal changes will deliver aspects—or some form—of desirable radicalism, always amorphous, always metaphysical, always deliberately slippery and far-off in the distance. This is the passive approach that constantly avoids direct engagement and action. There is an emphasis on talking around the edges of revolutionary change, but forever shying away from real radical changes, for they can never condone radical changes, let alone revolution. But they can, with spite and defensiveness, lambast the follies of radicalism and socialism. This position demonstrates a strong attachment to the capitalist and imperial system with all of its attendant social and racist dimensions. This approach is not the drive toward revolution, but rather a hunger for reforms that can, if implemented, avert revolution. At the center of this metaphysical imagination and construction is an ardent effort to maintain a constant distance between the progressives and the poor and the working class. Relying on an elitist position, in keeping with the social and class hierarchy in these imperialist societies, the progressives come to assume that they can speak on behalf of the poor and the oppressed—the poor that they do not know, and they have never really sought to know.

This matter becomes even more complicated when you add to the mix the issue of race. The progressive movements still suffer from the race question. At the moment, it would be fair to say that progressivism does not preclude racism. One can be relatively progressive on the environment and yet still remain an incorrigible racist. One can be a feminist, strenuously advocating for the advancement of white women, and yet still be a racist.

Part of the problem here has been endemic lack of, or avoidance of, ideological clarity and determination. In many cases this has involved courageously advocating for small incremental changes (sometimes on the very edges of the system), but never calling into question the capitalist, racist, imperialist system itself.

Progressives have also been known to discount the linkage between the local and the global and to downplay the need for effective solidarity with the oppressed and exploited victims of imperialism in the Global South. Quite often, US imperial incursions overseas have been supported (or explained away) by many who ordinarily regard themselves as progressives. In other words, their progressivism has tended to be very localized, sometimes very "tribal" or confined to specific internal, domestic causes. In refusing to see the aggression, destruction, exploitation, and oppression of US imperialism overseas, these progressives have turned their backs on the poor and oppressed in the Global South and even within their own country. Here we have, therefore, the curious and troubling existence of progressives in support of imperialism.

The pursuit of reforms as a strategy for liberation in Africa falls and disintegrates into unsalvageable parts when confronted by the unrelenting and unyielding brutality of neo-colonial regimes acting at the behest of imperialism. Even if some minor reforms are granted, and this rarely happens, such granting, in itself alone, would not lead to liberation. Neo-colonialism does not contain within it the capacity to reform and then become an anti-imperialist instrument of national liberation.

III

The strength of our commitment to the African revolution will be reflected in our willingness to endure; to remain persistent, steadfast, and focused. We enter on this journey fully aware that the desired results will not be immediately forthcoming. In fact, we must mentally and physically accept one thing: that we, the present generation, may not actually benefit from the struggle. That is, the results may come long after we have gone. What then can be considered as our singular contribution? That we were able to make this outcome, this African revolution, possible. We enter the struggle not for personal benefit or even vanity. We enter on this journey so that our people, if they remain true to the cause, can benefit from the fruits of liberation. In benefiting, they can live in peace and stability and enjoy the fruits of their labor in dignity without paying homage to imperialism. And, as Mao told the Chinese people in 1949, in achieving liberation, our people will have stood up, and in standing up, no one will dare insult us again. (See: Mao, "The Chinese people have stood up…nobody will insult us again," cited in: Han Suyin, *The Morning Deluge: Mao Tsetung and the Chinese Revolution, 1893-1954.* Boston/Toronto: Little Brown & Co., 1972, p. 498.) The principal objective of the African revolution is to make us, as Africans, stand up.

What we know is that no such liberation can occur outside of or separate from a coherent and organized revolutionary party. It is this party that will choose the appropriate strategy suitable to the historical moment and circumstances. Strategy is forged in response to circumstances, but the desired outcome remains the same: to oust imperialism from Africa. This inescapable desired outcome will influence the choice of strategy to be employed in the struggle.

Resistance against the African revolution must be anticipated. It will come from the local neo-colonial rulers and from the Western centers of the empire. Those embarking on this road must expect prompt and predictable resistance from local and foreign centers of imperialism. It is the revolutionary party that will hold the revolutionary struggle in place during moments of setbacks, and encounter with seemingly insurmountable hurdles.

All organized resistance against imperialism is, of necessity, many steps ahead of the oppressor. As far as possible, all actions and responses of the neo-colonial regimes must be anticipated and considered as those strategies of resistance are themselves formulated and continually revised. This cannot be done without the persistent guidance of the revolutionary party. Revolutionary resistance has what the oppressor regime does not have and can never have: the people. This is the indispensable ingredient, the crucial variable, for change. Success has to be seen as the byproduct of careful and appropriate marshalling of this power. There must be no rush to actions that expose people to unnecessary hardships and deaths. Such hardships and deaths must be in advance of the revolutionary struggle and not the result of impulsive miscalculations and vanity on part of the leaders. People will follow if they see themselves and their future reflected in the actions, aims, and examples of the leaders of the revolution. This support evaporates, or at least starts to evaporate, the moment the leaders are perceived to be inept, reckless, and lacking in ability and courage to plan the course of the revolution.

The initial stages of the revolutionary party in many African countries may in fact exhibit characteristics of a political coalition. This is not fatal. And we should not shy away from it as a building bloc in the drive toward the African revolution. It is the nature of coalitions to contain within them several political strands. Such coalition can only be considered as a strategic contribution to the African revolution if the total aggregate of its components is pointing to the desired future, that is, a valiant attempt at re-imagining the country beyond ethnic identity and regional loyalty. There must also be a clear and unwavering commitment to class analysis and to the identification of imperialism as the enemy. The components of the coalition must attract the forgotten, the poor, the marginalized, the struggling sections of society, the workers, the peasants, the landless, women, and those professionals who feel oppressed and excluded. This coalition has benefited from evident national class distinctions and also provided a framework for refined social class analysis as a basis of the national revolution.

Refinement of the coalition's ideological identity is absolutely crucial to the rise of a national revolutionary party. In order to lead, the revolutionary party must come to be identified with one ideology: socialism in pursuit of communism. The coalition cannot be allowed to remain amorphous and unwieldly for any extended period. If this happens, there is a clear danger of these progressive efforts falling apart into quarrelsome reactionary splinters catering to personal vanity and reactionary identities and therefore open to infiltration by agents of imperialism.

But won't the struggle for the African revolution lead to chaos and even instability? One reliable weapon wielded by the ruling classes in Africa is the call for unity and stability as defined by them. A self-serving myth has been popularized by these classes and their international allies, insisting that only repressive rulers can ensure stability in Africa; that Africans only respond to brutal strength. This is of course offensive, racist, and anti-historical. Yes, people everywhere yearn for peace and stability. But we also know that "peace under oppression" is not peace for the oppressed. This is the result of fear; of gritting one's teeth in internal anger and fury in order to endure and survive. As examples, we may look at the "peace" that prevailed under colonial rule, under slavery, and even under Apartheid. This was the everyday manifestation of repression, surveillance, punitive measures, meted out to anyone who dared to oppose; this was brutality in play. Claims by repressive regimes to be the guardians of peace and stability are hollow and fraudulent. What people desire is peace that is the consequence of social justice as an everlasting foundation.

In the drive toward the African revolution, we must resist the imperial inspired urge to quickly compromise with injustice for the sake of "peace and stability." We cannot allow injustice to be the defining characteristic of our societies. No one wants eternal strife, killings, warfare, and commotion. It is nonetheless incorrect to equate resistance to imperialism with the gratuitous embrace of violence and instability. In order to dislodge imperialism, there has to be resistance. And it is this resistance that is the inevitable midwife to social justice. A people mobilized, a people inflamed with righteous anger, a people walking with determination, cannot be stopped, or scared; they will not back down.

Since the 1960s, there is now an established strategy of the international community intervening in internal political quarrels in African countries. The justification for these several interventions is that the international community will come in as objective, fair-minded neutral arbiters. Over the years, "the international community" has come to mean Western powers, or the United Nations Organization (UNO), whose operations have tended to be dominated by Western powers. It is useful to remember that the West can never be—and will never be—neutral in these conflicts, especially if there are clear ideological differences among the parties. At the center of all Western thinking and actions are studied efforts to ensure its domination. At all costs, and in every instance, all political struggles will be viewed through the prism of

Western self-interest. This explains perceived delays in intervention in some conflicts or merely tepid efforts at intervention in others. We make a big mistake in imagining that the West will ever act to protect local African interests at the expense of imperialism. We must start on this journey toward the African revolution fully aware that conflict with the West is, after all, inevitable.

As we enter this decisive phase of our future, we must forever remember to acknowledge and elaborate upon the Pan-African and international dimension of our struggle. That is, our struggle for liberation cannot be attained without linking it to other struggles against imperialism around the world. Imperialism is, and has always been, the enemy. This observation does not by any means imply that we, in Africa, cannot embark on our struggle for liberation until the shots of revolution have been fired in other parts of the world, especially in the Global South. Not at all. What is self-evident is that our heroic struggles will both inspire and in turn receive fraternal solidarity from similar struggles, principally in the Global South. But this fraternal linkage does not—and cannot—delay the launching of our African revolution.

Understanding the Pan-African dimension of this revolution, is crucial to sustaining it in the current state of multiple, largely disunited neo-colonial countries on the continent. Since the late 1960s, there have been very few political parties formed in these countries with an avowed socialist program. Oginga Odinga's Kenya People's Union (KPU) was, in many respects, the last example of a radical nationalist party with ideological leanings toward socialism that sought to institute a radical ideological change in an African country using a pre-existing institution: the ballot.

The experience of the KPU in Kenya left behind several vital lessons. First, it is quite possible to create, organize, and sustain a class-based radical political party in African countries. Though short-lived (formed 1966, banned in 1969), Odinga's (and for some time, Kaggia's) efforts demonstrated a heroic watershed moment in Kenya's and indeed Africa's political struggle against imperialism. KPU was a valiant effort to realign national politics along class lines away from "tribalism"; an unsteady amalgam of the poor, dis-enfranchised, landless, squatters, ex-freedom fighters, unemployed, the oppressed, and the exploited across the country—that is, all those opposed to the avaricious ruling elite oppressing their fellow citizens as they eagerly "sold Kenya" to imperialism as the new collaborators. And this audacious effort, this daring experiment by Odinga almost worked. Even with all the power of the state, aided by Western governments (especially the UK and USA), use of government officials to deliberately subvert the constitution, even with all these disadvantages arrayed against it, the KPU almost won. Indeed, denied all access to the media, persecuted, harassed, hounded, and with minimal prior preparations and with limited resources, the KPU received more aggregate votes than Kenyatta's Kenya African National Union (KANU) in the "Little General Election of 1966." KANU won more seats in this hurriedly arranged election aimed at crippling Odinga's political power. Three years later, in 1969, Kenyatta forcibly banned KPU and threw Odinga into detention. The KPU, thus, had lost not because it was rejected by the people in the "arena of ideas," but rather due to brutal repression by a conservative ruling elite under Kenyatta, generously aided and controlled by the West.

The second lesson to emerge out of the KPU experience in Kenya relates to the suppression of isolated radical parties. Such isolation makes it easy to suppress and cripple a radical political party, let alone a revolutionary party, in any country in Africa. The KPU was isolated on the continent, and it was easy for key imperial powers to focus on it and its leader, Odinga. All the physical force and propaganda power of imperial countries and their local auxiliaries were trained on Odinga, and in this he stood no chance to survive. But this failure, in itself, also demonstrated the futility of seeking for radical changes from within. It also pointed to the inescapable need for intense preparation for the struggle, clarity of ideology, and a willingness to embark on a long, protracted struggle for social justice against imperialism. The KPU lacked the ability or facility to resurrect the struggle after the brutal encounter with forces of imperialism.

It is clear, therefore, that in order to survive and thrive, radical revolutionary parties will need to be formed and sustained across Africa. The struggle for the African revolution must be seen and conceived of as a Pan-African undertaking. It is necessary to mention here that this observation does not mean that there should be no revolutionary undertaking in single countries before the establishment of multiple revolutionary parties across the continent. Any such interpretation is deliberately misleading and counter-revolutionary. What is evident is that a multiplicity of revolutionary parties across the continent would facilitate fraternal solidarity, reinforce their commitment to radical Pan Africanism, and in the process make it difficult for imperial powers to quickly isolate and defeat them. A multiplicity of these revolutionary parties also, of course, points to an awakened continent. The planning, this time, must spring from the realization that this is going to be a people's protracted struggle against imperialism, with many inevitable setbacks along the way before the attainment of victory.

An integral part of any effort aimed at the launching of the African revolution is to study and understand the experiences of previous Marxist-inspired revolutionary movements in the 20th century. We must, with diligence and unsparing commitment, study and comprehend the nature and course of these revolutionary movements, in Africa and beyond. A tragic error on our part would be to bring to the table all the recycled and familiar anti-revolutionary verbiage emanating from Western mouths, pens, and keyboards. If indeed we want this African revolution to usher in our economic and even ideological independence, then we must see the world through our own eyes. We must seek to know the world through our prism. We have to collect the details, comprehend the course, provide our own analysis of the historical forces at play, and study the revolutionary leaders and policy formulations of each revolutionary party, and then their legacies. To this end, therefore, we should resolutely move away from the bourgeois impulse of condemning without comprehension. Such an impulse dutifully reinforces the power of the oppressive status quo.

The starting point in all these efforts is to pay attention to the Russian revolution, which occurred a little over one hundred years ago. No single event in the 20th century has been as consequential to the course of modern human history as the Russian revolution. There is hardly any aspect of our existence today that has not been touched by this revolution: from science, economics, or history to social sciences, literature, and social movements, etc. And, of course, the relative re-invention of Western societies to incorporate robust social welfare and amenities, in a bid to "contain the masses," is inescapably linked to the power of the example of the Russian revolution. We, in Africa, know that we partially owe our political freedom, *Uhuru*, to the direct forthright political and material support and, in international forums, from the Soviet Union. And even the Civil Rights Movement owes part of its success, in the post-1945 period, to the unrelenting criticisms of racism in the USA from the Soviet Union. All of this is now common knowledge. It is, therefore, vital for us to study in detail the rise and course of the Russian revolution. We should facilitate some of our young to specialize in the study of this revolution, and Russian Studies in general.

But why this emphasis? It was the first communist revolution in the world. It had no examples to emulate nor fraternal countries to come to its aid. It was born in a world hostile to it and to the ideology that it had brought into being. From its founding, the Soviet Union was marked for sabotage and destruction by the powerful Western powers and the world that they controlled. And this continued until 1991(and even beyond). Our detailed study will move us away from depending on Western interpretations of this revolution that brought into history "the alternative civilization." Another objective is to study the revolutionary initiatives of the Russian revolution. What was its starting point and what was the revolution able to achieve in spite of unrelenting Western hostility? Can these achievements be dismissed as inconsequential? What problems were encountered, and why? How did this revolution respond to questions of nationality, and how did it address the woman question, education, agriculture, industrialization, military conflicts? How was it able to survive and triumph over Hitler and his murderous Nazi regime? And how did this revolution serve as an endless inspiration to all subsequent Marxist revolutions, even while allowing for national and historical differences? What can we incorporate into our African revolution?

How do we educate ourselves? By first and foremost refusing to be held hostage by Western propaganda. It is not a mark of our cleverness, or a mark of being learned, to merely repeat what the West states about communism, and the Soviet Union, or Lenin, Mao and other revolutionary leaders of the 20th century. We cannot know the true nature of anything, of any subject, if all that we do is to look at someone else's notes. We can now read. Why do the ruling elite, the ruling classes, in the West hate communism so much? Why are they so afraid of communism? Do we, as Africans, share these fears? Can we really share these Western fears?

All modern revolutions in the 20th century and beyond were born in a world still dominated by modern imperialism. Efforts to chart out "the alternative civilization" were undertaken against the backdrop of pervasive world-wide racism, bigotry, established structures of exploitation, and oppression. These structures constitute the economic and cultural complex that holds the imperial system together. In terms of economic power, all revolutionary governments (and this includes the early years of the Soviet Union) were initially weak compared to the totality of power of the reigning imperial structure.

It has been repeatedly shown that the West, in a spirit of unforgiving vengeance, has sought and in many cases succeeded, to overthrow many of the revolutionary governments in the Global South who dared to enact secession from the imperial system. The West has the decisive voice in existing structures that control trade, commerce, and financial institutions. Control of current international trade routes and the structures that govern them, as well as financial institutions, remain durable weapons of-choice by imperialism against revolutionary change. Hence, all those trade linkages promoted under imperialism as evidence of free trade can quickly be converted to vengeful and spiteful weapons, whenever imperialism feels threatened. There is no free trade. There is no free enterprise.

In regard to the Soviet Union, Western scholars have been quick to point to its failures, especially to discrepancies between published aims and observable achievements. These critiques deliberately over-simplify historical realities, evade deep historical analysis, and assume the role of Western historical prosecutors out to condemn communism to a speedy death sentence. The reality is that, at the "moment of creation," the Bolsheviks had to respond to unparalleled internal crises in addition to fashioning new structures. The formulation (and shape) of policies and their implementation were all undertaken in the face of unrelenting Western real hostilities, internal residual resistance, scarcity of technical power and capital, and an urgent need to provide material benefits to a large and restive population in an expansive underdeveloped country reeling from decades of war and internal turmoil.

All Bolshevik leaders had hoped, in keeping with their belief in international revolution, that the spark of revolutionary change lit in Russia would, in short order, set off proletariat revolutions in Western Europe. And that these proletariat-led revolutions occurring in advanced capitalist countries, would in turn contribute to, and firmly participate in, the socialist reconstruction of Russia, Europe and beyond. It was anticipated that revolutionary Russia would be surrounded with fraternal solidarity from similar revolutionary movements and governments in Western Europe. This did not happen. By the time of Lenin's death on January 21st,1924, proletariat revolutions had yet to occur in Western Europe. Prospects for proletariat revolutions in Western Europe had dimmed. (See: E.H. Carr, *Studies in Revolution*, New York: The Universal Library, 1950, pp. 200-227.) This included Germany, where, until 1923, prospects for a proletariat revolution had momentarily seemed possible. Instead, what faced the Bolsheviks was a cordon of sustained hostility and counter-revolution being steadily and purposively constructed and extended around their country in a bid to both try and kill the ideology of communism in its bed, while at the same time severely limiting its spread beyond the borders of Russia. These unrelenting counter-revolutionary efforts took many forms, from: the military, economic and commerce, intelligence of multiple variety, propaganda, media, culture, intellectual, academic, religion, and deliberate mis-information. The subsequent rapid and consequential transformations that occurred in the Soviet Union from the 1920s, propelled communism from being just a dangerous idea, as seen by the ruling elite in the West, into a formidable foe and international threat to the hitherto unchallenged and undisturbed hegemony of Western imperialism. (See: Geoffrey Barraclough, *An Introduction to Contemporary History*, Harmondsworth, Middlesex, UK: Penguin Books, 1975. pp. 199-232.)

These details are mentioned not to exonerate or explain away any of the mistakes made, but rather to point out the greatness of the achievements attained, in spite of circumstances inherited by the revolutionary government, in: agriculture, industry, technology, education, infrastructure, health, the arts, women's liberation, military power, etc. This transformation was so historic that the country rose from economic and social backwardness to super-power status in less than sixty years, while overcoming internal resistance, Western continuous sabotage and hostility, and imperial wars of aggression, including Hitler's savage and murderous invasion. For a while, soon after *Uhuru*, many African governments were drawn to these achievements as possible models, before they were slapped on the wrist by the West and reprimanded for daring to admire the achievements of the enemy.

The unchanging position in the West has been to skip over these achievements and instead draw attention to their social cost. Western scholars and their allies in the intelligence agencies have been quick to discredit these achievements and point instead to what is characterized as their crudeness and their unforgiveable social cost— sullied, uncouth, not elegant, not admirable— that the price of these achievements was too high. Hence the consensus that Soviet achievements do not merit admiration. All of a sudden, however, these scholars and intelligence agencies have become fraternal comrades of the Soviet people. Their stated position is that, indeed, there were better (and natural) ways that could have been followed by the Soviet Union to achieve the same results, even if this would have taken a longer time. That the results would have been more elegant with limited social price. When they get here, this becomes an arena of dignified speculation. Western scholars and Cold War warriors and intelligence operatives, who have never led a revolutionary movement under constant attack, feel competent to provide alternative ways to implement socialist programs in a hostile world. They feel competent to advise on how revolutionary changes should have been instituted in the Soviet Union, in the crucial years between the 1920s and 1940s. The alternative method is, of course, the Western model of industrialization and economic growth, achieved over centuries, and presumed, therefore, to have inflicted less traumatic social cost on society.

But can we ever forget the centuries -old social cost of Western economic development? Whose social cost? Whose economic and political cost? Whose enduring death? Whose executions and multitudinous graves? Whose eternal oppression and humiliation? Whose discarded bodies, broken societies, permanently destroyed initiatives and hopes? Many of these Western scholars and intelligence agencies are unable to see the social cost of *Western* development, due to race and class and imperialism. The majority of them are white scholars (or intelligence functionaries) and, of course, many of them have endorsed the Western ideological hostility toward communism and the Soviet Union. They have no connection to peoples who have paid the ultimate social cost for the economic development of the West. This has not been a benign and harmless transformation. The painful trauma of this social cost has been a never-ending process over hundreds of years. Here, we can mention the enduring social cost shouldered by Africans and people of African descent in order to advance the rise of Western economic development, including industrialization. To this must be added the Native Americans and their near annihilation as a people in the Americas. How about the many holocausts endured by Africans? (Let us not forget the Congo under Leopold) And then there were the colonial wars of conquest, colonial policies, and reprisals against nationalist movements. All of these and more are indelible social costs shouldered by non-whites to advance this Western development routinely cited with pride by these scholars and intelligence agencies as a veritable weapon against communism and revolutionary movements.

Western scholars do not remember slave trade. They refuse to remember the social, political, and economic impact of the slave trade on Africa, and its corresponding positive impact on

Western development. They do not remember slavery and its enduring social impact. A social cost without any parallel. A social cost that has shaped world history and historical narratives even as it ushered in Western industrialization. A social cost that can never be repaid. How about the disaster that was colonialism, the bloody stranglehold of neo-colonialism, and the continued permanent under-development of the Global South? Modern imperialism is the living social cost that the oppressed and exploited still pay and endure to sustain Western development and material abundance. Billions of people locked in unending poverty, misery, violence, and oppression over centuries as they have remained victims of Western economic and political aggression. This suffering reinforces, on a daily basis, the power of imperialism and its ability to make the poor and the Global South pay for Western comfort, glamor, glitter, and delusion.

We, in Africa, we in the Global South, have, as a consequence of our dependence on the West, relied on our masters to interpret the world for us. We have relied on our masters to point out to us acceptable viewpoints to hold and propagate; acceptable theories and information to marshal to describe and explain the world around us and our place in it. Explanations that see the magnanimous nature of Western imperialism, and also its inevitable pathway as the shining light to our development. Theories that either by-pass imperial plunder and oppression or exonerate it of any notable blame for our permanent agonizing poverty, underdevelopment, and powerlessness. Our education, all filled with notable credentials, has ensured that in the end we know what we have been let to know, and we hate and abhor what our masters hate. We applaud what our masters applaud. We walk behind the master or on paths he has selected for us. And so, our hatred of communism is the product of cultural imperialism, education, Christianity (mainly) and other religions, colonialism, neo-colonialism, and calculated self-interest to avoid being labelled a "trouble-maker," so that we can be considered for the miniscule opportunities available in our midst. Obedient and elegant, fully in support of our positions and what they command.

Imperialism has, without any sense of shame, insisted that all those under its control must celebrate its achievements. These achievements comprise a severely edited version of its past, which is then taught and expected to be memorized from generation to generation. Contained in this glistening package are celebrations for imperial overlords, former slave traders and slave masters, homicidal racists, war mongers, defenders of class oppression, perpetrators of holocausts in the Global South, empire builders, robbers, purveyors of glamor, etc. Merit is seen and hailed in the actions of these plunderers, murderers, and slave masters. Power dictates that the oppressed must swear allegiance to this self-serving edited version of the imperial past, internalize it, and then celebrate it. Western scholars have found it reasonable and legitimate to explain away (by deliberate and forthright excision), the bone-chilling crimes of these empire builders, slave masters, captains of industry, founding fathers, and the glamor of their expansive social and material achievements. These are heroes of the West. These are revered pillars of the system. It has been one of the central tenets of Western imperialism to insist that all those under its domination must, without reservation, demonstrate respect and reverence for these heroes of the West.

On the other hand, Western scholars (and politicians) have, with relentless consistency, found communism and communist leaders to be without virtue; a system and its leaders with no identifiable redeeming virtue at all. Virtue resides in capitalism and imperialism. Heroes of the West always evince virtue. Heroes of the West either have no massacres, plunder, or genocide to their name or, if they do, all these can be easily explained away, and these explanations must be seen as rising in goodness above communism. Truth and morality are the preserve of imperialism. Goodness comes from the loins of imperialism. Communism is the inherent depository of all that is evil; of all that is objectionable in human civilization.

Education, academia, think tanks, funding agencies, armed forces, police, politics, religion, mass entertainment, media, corporate business, official policies, and imperial propaganda have ensured that this position remains pervasive and supreme, dominant, and largely unchallenged in the West and in the countries under Western hegemony. Under careful, deliberate cultivation, guidance, punishment, and reinforcement, these efforts have in turn produced unquestioned beliefs on the horrors of communism: no further need for elaboration, history, and justification. Now, the constant objective is to re-state, as irrefutable evidence, that communism is evil, that it has failed due its inherent ineptitude. And that this is abundantly obvious, even though it requires constant reinforcement and refurbishment.

These beliefs are now routinely relied upon to anchor the unchallenged structures of oppression, exploitation, and discrimination in the world under imperial domination. Not surprisingly, the oppressed and exploited do in fact declare their allegiance to these beliefs and, on cue, recite them as evidence of loyalty to capitalism and imperialism. Over hundreds of years, they have died in droves in grinding poverty and misery while expected to recite, to their grave, the virtues of the free enterprise system.

Part of the African agenda for liberation, is to refuse to accept imperialism's self-portrayal and self-narrative as true. We must insist on constructing a separate and different portrayal of imperialism. We are not looking at the same past and, therefore, we cannot identify the same heroes. We are not liberated on account of our dazzling knowledge and details about the heroes of our oppression and exploitation. Reciting the glamor of the master does not constitute our liberation. Different past, different analyses, values, and conclusions. Different past, different heroes. Different past, different future. And we must look at imperial achievements as products of hundreds of years of terror, violence, and trauma visited upon on our societies, and our resultant on-going oppression and exploitation. We are students of the permanence of oppression, violence, and exploitation.

IV

Going forward, the realization of the African revolution will rely heavily on the inevitable and historic linkage between the revolutionary elite and the oppressed masses. That revolutionary elite will have to provide leadership to the national liberation. The principles and values guiding the revolution will be articulated by the revolutionary party. Leadership will, therefore, be denied to all those intent on reproducing the failed and harmful neo-colonial solutions and cultures. The energy, the ideas, the tempo must emerge from the oppressed and the exploited masses. The revolutionary elite, fired by a burning commitment to the rebirth of their country and continent, must win the trust of the politicized masses imbued with a revolutionary ideology.

This historic linkage, this revolutionary outcome cannot arise if the revolutionary elite are unconnected to the workers in the cities and the peasants in the rural areas. The worst thing that can happen to the revolutionary cause is to have intellectual Africans who distance themselves from Africa. That is, Africans who talk endlessly about Africa in bourgeois terms, but who have no visible or sustained connection to rural Africa. If we do not know the rural areas intimately, then we have essentially abandoned Africa. The majority of our people still reside in the rural areas. The values of Africa, even if under threat from forces of globalization, are most evident there. The meaning of underdevelopment, poverty, social neglect, and political ruthlessness under imperialism is visible for all to see in the rural areas.

This also includes the inescapable struggle for women's liberation. A distinctive feature of the African revolution is the embrace and advocacy of women's liberation. There can be no true African revolution without women's liberation, not as a perfunctory and incidental addition to the program and platform, but as an integral definition of the liberation struggle. To advance an African revolution independent of women's liberation is to reconstitute banditry, corruption, oppression, violence, and then to disown the centerpiece of social justice and equality. The struggle for women's liberation cannot exclude women as liberators, part of the national revolution, seated at the table in the formulation of ideas and positions infused in the revolutionary party.

The danger has been for the bourgeois elite to relate to the rural areas as foreigners, dashing in to make brief strategic forays and then dashing out, in the manner of a colonial official touring native areas and then hurrying out to get back to "civilization." The nature and type of this interaction has been laced with imperial overtones. We must affirm that we cannot comprehend the true injurious nature of imperialism in Africa without paying serious attention to the rural areas. We seek to know, not to be praised or hailed. We seek to know through humility and dedication as part of the revolutionary struggle against imperialism.

A big and unforgiveable mistake would be for the revolutionary elite to assume a colonial posture—to appear as the learned expert lecturing to the ignorant masses. This would immediately kill all efforts toward the African revolution. It would also sour the masses against any talk of revolutionary change.

It is expected that the revolutionary elite will study and listen. Study, explore, and discuss. Study and observe. Record, revise, study, revise. Reaffirm, commit, organize, build, be humble in approach but remain steadfast and focused. And then, and only then, outline correct practices. Ask. Educate. Explain. Discuss. Prepare. Launch. Always look at the struggle from a long-term perspective.

Before this can happen, the revolutionary elite will need to extricate themselves from several political, cultural, and even economic webs and traps. We cannot run away from the fact that part of the hold and attraction of imperialism on and over the educated elite in the Global South, in Africa, lies in its power. This power has an intoxicating, disabling aroma, that draws the educated elite to imperialism. They admire this power, they covet this power, they salivate over this power. They want to be part of this power. And by the theory of association and reflected glory, they see themselves as powerful because of their loyalty and proximity to imperialism. They yearn to be noticed, to be honored, to be identified, to be mentioned, to be elevated above those who have resisted or have no credentials. To such an educated elite, the purpose of their existence is to affirm the power of imperialism and not sabotage or resist it. They know that imperialism will not celebrate its critics and that those who resist will be overlooked, sidestepped, and sidelined. And reprisals will, in bundles, repeatedly knock on their doors. Many of these educated elite have even been active participants in the construction and maintenance of the neo-colonial enterprise.

There was a moment in the early years of *Uhuru*, in many African countries, when it was speculated that the training of local Africans at university level and in advanced technical education would enhance and facilitate development; that this training would solve the endemic problem of lack of trained personnel and administrators. It was also speculated that part of the reason why there had been a "false start" in Africa was because many of the "founding fathers" lacked advanced academic training; and that, from the start, these leaders had been unable to fully comprehend the complexities of modern commerce, economics, education, etc. Also, it was thought that lowly educated leaders tended to be corrupt, narrow-minded, rigidly backward-looking, and ever so "tribal." The record of more than fifty years of *Uhuru* provides a disturbing roll call, an alarming report card, especially for the educated elite. We have now had thousands of educated Africans enter government in various layers of administration and power. The results have been disappointing. For the most part, these educated Africans are just as corrupt, ruthless, "tribal," and supremely pro-imperialism as the lowly educated leaders. Education alone is not the answer.

The educated elite have joined the looting with vigor, by providing expertise in these acts of naked treason. In other words, higher education has not slowed down the neo-colonial business. If anything, education has accelerated its implementation and expansion in African countries. As much as education has led these educated elite "to be somebody," it has not facilitated the economic and cultural liberation of Africans. The crux lies in the purpose of this education and its expected outcomes. Under neocolonial conditions, education promptly reinforces imperial laden values. It deepens dependency and thus cannot be relied upon to challenge the structure of neo-colonialism. The overarching social, political, and economic values reinforce the imposed neo-colonial attitudes and dispositions. These include wholesale admiration of the Western economic structure (in design and values) and of Western cultural productions, etc. The purpose is simple: a reproduction of, or at least an attempt to reproduce the West in these countries.

Still, the revolutionary elite will emerge from these conditions embracing the Western cultural domination that produces confusion and even self-degradation. They will, through the valiant efforts of the revolutionary party, focus on education for liberation, thus moving from the educated elite to the revolutionary elite. And in this, it will be clear that the education, the knowledge that liberates us, cannot simultaneously celebrate and endorse the virtues of imperialism. We have, therefore, to draw a distinction between vanity in the service of imperialism, and education for liberation. We must see the differences between education for individual glory and education aimed at exposing the crimes of imperialism and at preparing the society and the people for their liberation.

As a people struggling for our liberation, we should remember that, for us, all worthwhile scholarship must, of necessity, be oppositional to imperialism. We cannot restart our societies under imperialism. Our future cannot find footing under imperial domination. Our cultures, our creativity, our economies, our science and scientific inquiries, all of these cannot find originality, sustenance and rejuvenation under imperial domination. The basic focus of the patriotic intellectuals in Africa (and the Global South generally) must be the attainment of liberation from imperial domination. The attainment of degrees alone is not enough. Pursued as an end, academic degrees can be the enemy. Degrees that reinforce the power of imperialism cannot be seen as a positive contributory factor toward our liberation. Learned praises for imperialism and its positive contributions to Africa and to the Global South are anthems to our death in oppression. What has been evident is that the quest for individual glory in the service of imperialism does little to expose its crimes, past and present. Our scholarship must lead us to establish meaningful solidarity with our people: the oppressed and exploited.

This introduces the delicate matter of the relationship between African intellectuals and their Western allies, Western liberal scholars who, on the surface, may seem well disposed toward Africa. We must at once acknowledge that this relationship has, in the past and in the present, been a source of ideological confusion. Pointing to a nebulous liberal future, Western scholars have tended to shy away from revolution and radical Pan-Africanism: too radical, too revolutionary, too black. Can African intellectuals committed to our liberation and Western liberal scholars ever have identical aims? For the Western liberal scholar (mostly white), knowledge of Africa is not premised on agitating for the continent's liberation from the shackles of imperialism. It can be a career, a fascination, an opportunity to shine, an indulgence, etc. In other words, the future of Africa is not a burning question for the white Western liberal scholar. They can still be authorities on Africa, even as Africa sinks. For the patriotic African scholar, the fundamental aim is to prevent Africa from sinking. To be sure, this can be part of a career in scholarship, etc. But the mission is different.

Western liberal scholars have been unwilling, and perhaps unable, to forthrightly condemn Western imperialism and its plunderous and murderous habits across the world. They have been willing to describe and annotate instances (even pervasiveness) of poverty and oppression in the Global South. But their explanations and remedies routinely avoid condemning imperialism. These explanations amount to a mouthful of confusion, a labyrinth of incoherence. In the end, they are still children of the West. To be taken seriously by their colleagues in the West, these liberal- scholars side-step radical Marxist analysis of imperial plunder.

There is, therefore, a limit beyond which Western liberal scholars cannot go. For all their eloquence and well-rehearsed phrases, white liberal scholars are stuck on the identity of race and loyalty to the West. They speak in general terms about social justice and progressive politics. But that is where it ends. White liberal scholars are not able to cross the river. They can never fully identify with Africans and other oppressed peoples in the Global South. They abhor radical politics and, together with conservatives, they loathe any mention of socialism, let alone Marxism. They are wedded to the system. And as much as they may disagree with a few details in the system, they embrace the prevailing social, economic, and political structure. They are unable to see that this system, this structure, is destined to repeatedly produce these injustices that they comment on in ever expanding publications and narrations.

No matter how close the personal relationships might be between the Western liberal scholars and the African revolutionary intellectuals, in the end they break and lie scattered on the floor whenever communism and the Soviet Union are subjects of discussion. We can only be tolerated in the room if we take the Western flags to denounce the Soviet Union and its many unforgiveable mistakes. We are good if we provide obedient muscle behind Western denunciation of communism and radical nationalism. On this matter, like many others, Western liberal scholars assume the position of the educated elite talking to the uninformed in the Global South. Their conclusions, inspired by an abiding ideological need to defend capitalism and imperialism, are framed as clinically objective without any ideological connection, as driven by facts. Those who resist, those who refuse to bow and salute, are dismissed as ignorant and ill- informed demagogues prone to spewing out irresponsible polemics.

One of the unmistakable signs of the crime of imperial cultural domination of the Global South is the suppression of local original voices agitating for liberation. What neo-colonialism does is to punish local voices of resistance and then proceed to sow seeds of doubt among the dominated. This leads the dominated to doubt the value of their own thoughts. Can they really be original? Can they be seen as original before the West confers this title on them? Who will listen to them? Western liberal scholars, descendants of the colonizers, are very much aware of this. They know that, under the guiding hand of imperialism, they can impose their intellectual domination on these peoples. After all, they have come to reckon that in this imperial world, Western liberal scholars set trends and invent merit. Not surprisingly, on many occasions the dominated sit and wait for these descendants of the colonizers to arrive and make pronouncements. Imperial power and prestige ensure that their pronouncements are rarely "thrown out of the house." Of all the maladies issuing from colonialism and neo-colonialism, this is the most vile and insidious.

Self-doubt, which leads to insecurity among the oppressed and dominated, conspires against internal cooperation and nurturing of local talent. Instead, there emerges intense internal personalized rivalries and competition for notice and power, and even vanity. Their training and apprenticeship at the feet of Western oracles have left the oppressed to believe that the local cannot be original, cannot peer into the future, cannot arrive at conclusions that merit attention. Sharpest criticisms are hence aimed at the local, at each other. Criticisms against Western scholars and their output will remain evasive, tentative, and circumspect, criticisms that do not offend or cause discomfort.

And it must be pointed out, for emphasis, that these Western liberal scholars have monopolized and dominated writings on Africa; that they have, in the past and the present, shaped the nature and direction of African Studies. This domination has come to include definitions and meanings of our history, emphasis, historical pain, suffering, genocide, exploitation, holocausts, poverty, and even the future. And to this must be added the guiding hand and resources that shape "nuanced outcomes" and determine acceptable pronouncements. It can safely be argued that we have, as Africans, "known ourselves" through the eyes of liberal Western scholarship on Africa. It is a position that they have, with energy and creativity, sought to uphold.

Partly out of racial arrogance and a sense of entitlement, Western liberal scholars have become accustomed to making final and authoritative pronouncements on Africa. This is the phenomenon of what can be termed the Imperial Imperative, which ensures that Western liberal scholars have reserved seats on any intellectual issue, especially if it affects Africa and the rest of the Global South. They automatically occupy a privileged position. They are the serious scholars, forever travelling in the company of sophisticated analysis—the real investigators, the serious scientists, the inventors. Their pronouncements are given attention. Their claims to originality, to original formulation of ideas, to creating new knowledge, are rarely doubted. Thus, they enjoy enormous advantages by virtue of being descendants of the imperial center. They have access to advantages that can never be open to the dominated, the oppressed, and the exploited. Scholars from the dominated groups and societies must prove that they belong, that they can ever belong. Western liberal scholars have pre-paid membership to this club of privilege and power. They are permanent members of the executive board of this club. Their abiding duty is to defend its borders.

As part of the Imperial Imperative, the products of the labor of Western liberal scholars are accorded more inestimable value than similar works and contributions from the ranks of the dominated. They own the system, including paths to rewards and avenues to recognition. The system, the world, is rigged for them. This is Imperial Imperative.

We know that this sense of imperial posturing is not limited just to scholars. Relationships between citizens of the imperial countries and citizens of the dominated countries conform to this pattern. In their behavior, citizens of imperial countries assume imperial attitudes. They are variously loud, haughty, condescending, arrogant, entitled, scornful, dismissive. They demand and expect deference and obedience from the dominated peoples. Their behavior is modelled on the colonial era officials and missionaries. They deride the oppressed. They despise them.

A definite mark of powerlessness, of being dominated, is having one's history, experiences (and condition), defined, characterized, and described by outsiders; by foreigners who until recently ruled you. At the moment, we in Africa, are still a people whose historical narratives and life experiences are largely shaped and determined from outside. This distinction, odd and colonial, has definite social, cultural, political, and economic implications on our quest for liberation, for revolution. Resistance to this enterprise must be one of the signature assignments of the African revolutionary elite. It would be mischievous to conclude that this resistance constitutes building a wall around Africa and thus excluding non-Africans from undertaking scholarly inquiries on the continent. Not at all. But we must concede, as a matter of urgency, that an integral part of our liberation consists of Africans defining Africa, of Africans being authorities on the African revolution.

The rise of globalization, the "world as a village," the modern world, and other innocent-sounding bourgeois terminologies and concepts have not softened the piercing force and sustained pervasive power of imperialism in our societies. We have been part of this integrated capitalist and imperial system for centuries. What is remarkable, what is painful for us to see, is that in all this time, in all these centuries, our roles have not changed. Imperialism has been unable to explain this consistency of our poverty and oppression. Continuous integration into the imperial system has led to our unshakeable poverty and powerlessness. Terminologies have changed, but our condition has remained the same. We are still the impoverished abused laborers in the house of imperialism over centuries. We are still the poorest of the poor. Our lands and oceans are still plundered by imperialism, so rich in resources and yet so very poor. We are still the excluded, the despised, the oppressed.

We are aware of the fact that, even at this moment in history, when Western imperialism is unsteady and largely in decline, it is still lethal and inventive in modes of survival. The ruling classes in Western countries, have, at this period, inherited an imperial outlook alongside dwindling fortunes. These ruling classes have inherited an imperial complex and reflex, an imperial framework, readily deployed in dealing with oppressed people, other societies, and international problems. They are the proud inheritors of past imperial examples of domination and a legacy that they seek to defend and uphold. This is their natural recourse: resort to imperial posture and use of force and constant threats of economic reprisals to enforce compliance. The West has lost the argument; it must limp along on the strength of its armed forces and current domination of international routes of commerce. And so, even as circumstances have seemed to change, these ruling classes remain under the seductive influence of past glory. They walk through this moment in history with their eyes fixed onto the past. They aim for endless imperial power, glamor, and glory. They issue orders, invade poor countries, demand obedience, and use imperial-laden vocabulary to describe their enemies: heathens, lunatics, uncivilized, barbarians, fanatics, undemocratic, monkeys, etc. This attitude refuses to see any rationale for resistance against imperial overlordship.

To the ruling classes in the West, the world is normal and just and stable when imperial power is unchallenged. In other words, perpetual oppression, and exploitation at home, and then mostly in the Global South, is deemed normal and just and even fair. Operationally, this state of imperial normalcy, this stability, is predicated upon the continued existence of a non-industrialized and, therefore, a non-competitive Africa and the rest of the Global South. Rulers of imperial countries accustomed to issuing orders and making demands on the poor and the weak, are inherently unable to devise a non-imperial world. They simply cannot. For this to happen, there would need to be a dialogue between the West and the Global South to discuss the state of the world on an equal footing. The West would, for once, have to listen. But this will not happen. To be able to listen, you must respect the speaker. Imperialism has never respected those under its domination.

To maintain its wealth and power (and then its polished rationalizations), the West must keep in place the poverty and powerlessness of the people of the Global South, preferably, in their own countries, away from the West. Capitalism will cease to exist the moment there is no poverty and powerlessness in the Global South. There cannot exist, nor will there be, the co-existence of a developed Global South and developed imperial centers. The rise of the Global South free from oppression and exploitation must, of necessity, spell the doom of imperialism. For then, there will be no Global South. We must be careful to mention here that we are talking of developed societies free from imperial control and exploitation. This is different from sporadic provision of water and even elementary schooling to an increasing number of people. This is different from the pitiful ambitions of some countries to be elevated as "middle-income" on the imperial totem pole. "Middle-income countries," forever dubious and slippery, are still under the yoke of imperialism. The danger here is to imagine that imperialism ceases to exist if the poor in the Global South, in Africa, can get two or even three meals a day and a blanket. Should all the struggles for liberation be suspended and even abandoned simply because the oppressed and the exploited have reasonable access to water and clothing? Why have these elementary necessities been difficult to attain in all these many tortured centuries?

A resounding big obstacle to our liberation lies lodged in the temptation to be seduced by false gestures, by empty glistening gestures. History teaches us that the object, the living object, of struggles for liberation is not to be less oppressed, to be less exploited, to be less humiliated, to be less discriminated against. The enduring object, the inalterable object of these struggles, is to *end* oppression and exploitation, and to *expel* imperialism from our lives and our societies. The comprador class looks at some alleviation of poverty as being the equivalent of liberation. We do not seek for blankets and donated foods as the end of our struggle. We do not seek for imperial charity as our definition of liberation. Liberation, as defined by us, and not by our oppressors and exploiters, cannot co-exist with imperial oppression and exploitation. This is the enduring lesson of history.

Imperialism cannot reform itself out of existence. These rulers and the system they preside over cannot endorse a world based on equality of peoples. Inevitably, therefore, the future that they champion, and advocate, is a replication of the imperial past (and present). Their desired future is their glorious imperial past. The West must continue to rule and dominate. No think tanks, universities, rulers, or op-ed pieces can envision a world not ruled and dominated by the West. This is why our future does not, and cannot, lie under the umbrella of imperial domination. There is no liberation for us under imperialism. There will never be freedom, development, and liberation for us under imperialism.

The African revolution is an emphatic refusal, on our part, to continue to accept subordinate roles under imperialism. This revolution provides for Africa a people-centered and people supported march towards economic independence and the genuine start on the gigantic task of controlling its natural resources, the ownership, access, and utilization of these resources. The African revolution will defend us as a people. It will celebrate the multiplicity of our cultures and languages. Consequently, we will resist all external cultural influences that denigrate our cultures, our values, and our persons. Also, this revolution will unleash the creative potential of artists, writers, scholars. The African revolution has an inescapable obligation to create a caring society, a reciprocal society, a dignified society, an independent society: a society with openly accountable leaders under the guidance of the revolutionary party.

In 1964, Chou En-Lai, the Prime Minister of the People's Republic of China, under Mao, proclaimed in Tanzania that Africa was "ripe for revolution." This led to hurried, brutal, and nervous dismantling of any sign of national radicalism and socialism in Africa by neo-colonial leaders under the command of imperialism. Since 1991, Africa has been silent on the question of organized radical revolutionary change. There are, of course, isolated intellectuals and groups that still hold onto the dream of revolution in Africa. At this moment in our history, prospects for revolution in Africa are continually enhanced by the excesses of imperial exploitation and oppression: economic deprivation and crushing poverty; unemployment; agricultural mismanagement and landlessness; marginalization of groups and communities; women's oppression and gender discrimination;

child labor; "stealing of elections" and political impunity; racism against Africans on their own soil; the punishing outcomes of cultural imperialism; lack of respect for us as Africans; massive corruption; extreme income and wealth gap between the rich and the poor; lack of housing; brutality and oppression; underfunded, undefined, and disorganized education and training; grossly inadequate health care and medical expertise; destruction of the environment; rapid depletion and waste of the continent's natural resources; "selling of the country" to imperialism; and cultural strangulation and domination by the West. All these and more provide credible launching pads for radical movements on the continent. Now, more than ever, Africa is indeed, "ripe for revolution."

INDEX